BEFORE

layla Audeamus

ISBN: 979-8-88945-021-4
eISBN: 979-8-88945-022-1

Brilliant Books Literary
137 Forest Park Lane Thomasville
North Carolina 27360 USA

Printed in the United States of America

ACKNOWLEDGEMENTS

For a dear, sweet friend who helped to steer me in the right direction;

The loves who are no longer here but the one who came and rescued me from a formless, Masterless existence, I've given my body, behavior, and attitude and you accepted.

DOWN TIME

Alice looked at the newest magazine in the stack and didn't find it particularly impressive. Her patience was wearing thin and the fact the doctor was so tardy didn't help matters. She was not used to waiting so long to see the old family friend who was also their family doctor.

Waiting for anything was not something Alice had ever found necessary. Her parents and the endless parade of nannies, companions, and 'keepers' her family had hired had done what she wanted, when she wanted. Waiting, that was for others to do, not her. She had about decided that staying in this generic waiting room was not necessary when her name was finally called.

"Alice Blake, Alice Blake, the doctor will see you now." The dumpy little nurse stood at an open door with her chart and had called her name. She might as well see the doctor; it would finally get her aunt off her back about taking care of her health. For every semester she had been living with her aunt and working on her master's degree, she would lose as much as five pounds because of her eating habits and auntie wasn't sure if she wasn't putting her health at risk by her failure to eat regularly.

Alice stood, took her bag, and coat before following the nurse through the open door. The inner office smelled of disinfectant and a popular pine based cleaner. The woman wanted her to get on the scale and her height and weight was noted in her medical record. "Come this way, it's the third door on the left," the nurse said.

"Great" she thought to herself. First the interminable wait in the outer room and now another in the exam area. The nurse took her blood pressure, temperature, and asked her about medications. The nurse's part of the torture was over and she left.

Alice had good reason for not liking doctor's offices. Both her mother and father had died from cancer and it had all started in a doctor's office. In fact, the man she was seeing today had been her mother's doctor until surgeons, oncologists, and finally hospice people had taken her over.

"Alice, Alice," the soft voice of her family doctor finally pierced the reverie she had been having with herself.

"Uh, oh, yes, Doctor Salek, thank you for seeing me." Alice had to pay attention and she needed to think of the here and now, not the past.

Dr. Salek looked down her chart while asking her why she had come to see him. "Any problems or issues? How are you getting on with your Aunt Dorie?"

"Aunt Dorie is okay, I don't like being away from my friends here in Oakland, but then many of them are off at University now." She softened to the doctor a bit; he really was a nice old guy. "I don't regret not leaving town to go to University, but I do miss my old house."

"Well, everything looks good on your chart. I know the death of your mother and having to move to Green Valley to stay with your aunt can't have been pleasant, but you're a strong girl and it will all work out in the end." The doctor looked at her file for a last time and started to leave. He turned back, "if you ever meet a young doctor named Khoury in Green Valley, you might want to steer clear. He has a bit of a reputation and it's not all good." He shook Alice's hand and saw her out of the office.

Alice was glad to get away from the medical center where Dr. Salek had his practice. Oakland had been Alice's home until her mother's death had necessitated her move to Green Valley. The forty-five-minute drive from her old home in Lindsey Road to Aunt

Dorie's small bungalow in Green Valley wasn't so much about distance but about scale. The large family home she had grown up in had been sold and the money put into a trust fund for her. Where once she had a spacious room which was constantly kept clean by servants, she now lived in a small room which her aunt thought she should be responsible for keeping tidy. Alice looked forward to the day when her degree was finally finished and she could leave her aunt's house for good.

Growing up, Alice had few interests that stuck with her for longer than a few days or months. Her mother had forced her to take piano lessons, dancing classes, and riding lessons when she was a child, but she didn't practice the piano, hated dancing, and when she found out that the stables where she was taking the riding lessons expected her to saddle, unsaddle, and care for the horse, she refused to go back. The one thing that she did like from her childhood was her friendship with Evie Marsh.

Evie's real name was Elvira but she hated it and being a good friend, Alice joined her in not liking the name. The Marsh family lived near Alice and getting to and from her friend's house was easy. Evie was in the same university as Alice, but her major, Latin, was different from hers.

Alice had always been and still was fascinated by the Middle Ages. Now, with finishing her Master's in History with a concentration on the Middle Ages firmly in site, she could see the day when her education would be finished, she could claim her inheritance, and move out of her aunt's house. Alice didn't have any plans to use her degree, but just having that one thing accomplished was somehow important to her.

Alice's mother had been sick when she started university and although there was staff in the house to care for her, Alice's mother had wanted her daughter to live at home. When the reading she had to do in one of her classes needed to be done, Alice would sit in her mother's sick room and read to her or just be with her mother while she read the tomes to herself. If she was close to anyone, it was her mother she was closest to and watching her slide further and further into the ravages of cancer, was not easy on Alice.

The drive back to her aunt's house seemed over long but with the time of day and traffic, it exasperated Alice. Any chance of a quite evening was turned into a fuse that any bump in her life would light and an explosion of temper would surely follow. After parking in the driveway, Alice sat in the car for a few minutes to calm herself, her aunt would be home and it wasn't fair to take her frustrations out on her relative.

Aunt Dorie was in her rocker by her knitting basket. She shouted a 'hello' to her great-niece as Alice walked through the door. Dorie was hard of hearing and like many people with that problem, raised the volume of her voice to overcompensate. Alice had learned that for her aunt to 'hear' her it was best to stand where her mouth could be seen. Dorie would never admit it, but much of her hearing was in fact, lipreading.

Alice's room was small compared to the large, airy one in her old house. School books, the many books she was expected to read for each of her classes or research papers, and the odd family photo graced the floor to ceiling bookcases on two walls of her room. The twin bed, dresser, a stool at the vanity table, were all that the room could hold. She no longer had a large private bath with her room, but shared the lone bath in the house with her aunt.

One more class and then the two semesters she would need to write her graduate thesis. This was all that stood between her and freedom. Heady stuff but first the last paper which was due by next Friday. Dr. Vincent's class on the prose of the late Middle Ages would take her attention for the next several days then she and Evie would be free for some serious beach time!

The Gulf of Mexico was warm, the waves lapped gently on the white sand beaches of Florida, and few people were out on the cloudy day Evie and Alice had chosen for the beginning of their between-term holiday. The beaches in this part of the country were not owned by private interests but were open to all. This area was popular with an older crowd who still respected people's privacy and found walking easier on the walkways that rimmed the beaches rather than on the sand.

The place chosen for their vacation was not far from where they both lived, but the atmosphere was light-years away. While they both liked quiet beaches, their eating and entertainment was another matter. The popular places people of their age frequented was where their time would be spent when not in the condo they had rented or the beach. Alice had not liked the dancing classes her mother had insisted she take but now she could dance the night away with the best of them.

Club Zoom was the place to be and Evie had gotten a friend to give her a VIP pass which was good for a week. With the pass, they would not have to stand in line, possibly to be turned away like some unfortunates, and it gave her and Alice a chance to have something to eat before clubbing. Most of the better clubs didn't really get going until after ten, but for those who had to take their chances on getting in, they always started filling up the place early.

The Surf Club was an old favorite of Alice's. She had been there to eat when her parents were alive and vacationing in this part of the Gulf Coast. It was a bit more upscale than most young people could afford, but Alice did have a stipend from the estate and since it was vacation, she didn't mind the expense.

The food, as always was wonderful and she and Evie were about to leave. A middle-aged couple sitting at the next table caught Alice's eye. The lady seemed to be in some kind of distress. Immediately Alice saw the tinge of blue on the woman's lips.

Alice came out of her chair and was at the woman's side. She wasn't breathing. Alice had learned some emergency first aid while caring for her mother and it looked like the lady had something in her throat which was keeping her from breathing. Alice put her arms around the woman and tried the Heimlich maneuver but it didn't work. She pulled the woman from the chair and laid her on the floor. Her husband also came to his wife's side.

Alice kneeled beside the woman's head and positioned it so she could probe her mouth. A fish bone had lodged in her throat and Alice's probing fingers was finally able to remove it. She began mouth-to-mouth but moved out of the way when the EMTs arrived and took over the woman's care.

Evie and Alice left as the EMT team was lifting the woman into an ambulance. The husband, who introduced himself as Alex Khoury, thanked her and Alice simply smiled. The girls were off to Club Zoom.

Evie's VIP pass to the Club also gave them access to the exclusive area of the place reserved for the best and most important clientele. Evie was dressed in a shimmery silver dress which accentuated her blond hair and long legs. Alice's little black dress showed off an ample bosom, tiny waist, and equally long legs. Her long brown hair had natural red highlights. The pair immediately attracted attention.

Neither Evie nor Alice was into the casual hook-up scene. Both girls had been raised to be more responsible about entanglements and one-night stands were not going to happen. Dancing however, was another thing. Evie ordered the drinks and Alice began to dance to the beat of the music.

The VIP area had its own dance floor and Evie and Alice began to sway to the sounds of techno beats. Alice felt a presence behind her and strong hands held her by the waist. Breaking free she turned and found a tattooed man grinning at her. Over the volume of the music, he asked her name. "Alice, but take your hands off of me! No one invited you to crash my friends and my party!"

The man retreated saying, "Bitch, who needs trouble!" Thankfully she saw him leave.

Evie and Alice laughed and continued to dance. It was getting late and the next day they would be leaving to go to the next stop on their vacation. They'd both had enough to drink.

Dawn had barely begun but Evie and Alice were awake, packed, and had loaded Alice's car for the drive to New Orleans. Evie had checked out of the condo-hotel the night before and they could simply leave. Alice took her travel coffee mug and Evie's mug to the coffee bar near the front desk to fill them up for the trip.

A middle-aged man was sitting behind the desk and called out to Alice. "Are you Miss Blake, Miss Alice Blake?"

Alice stopped and nodded, "Yes, why?"

"Oh," he said, "There is a message for you. It was here when I came on night duty." He handed Alice the note and she put it in her pocket. She filled the coffee mugs, put the cream and sugar, to each ones liking, and returned to the room.

Alice drove the first two hours and Evie did the rest of the trip. The remainder of their vacation was in New Orleans. A quaint old hotel less than of a block from Bourbon and Toulouse streets was run by a wonderful couple. He was the hotelier and she the chef. The food in the restaurant was always first-class and the suite Evie and Alice shared was beautifully appointed.

The note the night clerk had given Alice was still in her pocket, forgotten. The girls changed after checking in the hotel and the porter had deposited their suitcases in their rooms. The suite had two bedrooms with king-sized beds and a sitting room with a mini-bar. Snacks were also available, but neither girl could see a need for any.

The first stop was a restaurant for red beans and rice with one Hurricane to wash it all down. The place was known for its storm themed drinks and trying to drink more than one was not recommended. When Alice and Evie had turned twenty-one, their birthdays being only two months apart, Evie had driven them both to New Orleans to celebrate. The same hotel in the best location gave the girl's easy access to all of the bars and eateries. It was then Alice learned that trying to drink three Hurricanes in one sitting could be quick and easy but trying to stand up was another matter. Walking unaided was impossible. Evie helped her back to the room and just as quickly the drinks went down, they came back up even quicker. Alice had learned her lesson and Evie knew now she needed to move out of the way faster!

The girls walked through the French Quarter and then took a bus to the Garden District. Evie was particularly interested in the Moore House gardens and the pair spent more than an hour enjoying the quiet paths around the property where the only sounds were the crunch of stones as they walked. Aunt Dorie's house didn't have a garden big enough to hold even one of the flower beds they saw laid out before them. Alice's old house, however, had ample space but no one to tend the plants. Once her father had died, Alice's mother had lost all interest in anything like that.

The plan was to go to Preservation Hall and sit on the hard seats to watch and listen to some original jazz as sung and played by the great artists who had come out of the New Orleans Jazz scene for more than a hundred years. Dinner would be after the show and probably from one of the many eateries which lined the main streets of the French Quarter. Neither Evie or Alice felt like changing after the tour of the Garden District and they were able to see the early performance at the Hall.

Dinner was a Po-Boy sandwich and a glass of white wine. Evie drank beer, but Alice could never stand the taste of it so she drank the wine. The girls finished their drinks as they strolled down Bourbon Street towards their hotel. A group of guys nearly collided with them and by their unsteady lurch into the street, it was obvious they'd drunk more than they could handle. One of the men tried to grab Evie but Alice pushed him aside.

Early the next morning, the pair went to the French Market to get hot chocolate and beignets. They climbed the stairs leading up to the top of the levee behind the Market and sat on a bench overlooking the Mississippi River. The traffic on the river was heavy and the two watched as tugboats, barges, and oceangoing ships passed going to and from the busy port.

Alice had made a reservation at the oldest restaurant in New Orleans, Antoine's. Established in 1840, it was French cuisine at its finest and their Baked Alaska desert worth waiting for. The evening was chosen almost a year ago because reservations were booked so far in advance. She had confirmed the time before they had left the beach and both girls were looking forward to dressing for dinner and the food.

The artists of Jackson Square were all showing their paintings and more than one was doing charcoal sketches of patrons who could pay the fee and sit for their portrait. The last time Evie had been in Jackson Square a lady did a caricature of her that wasn't very flattering or funny. Today, Alice decided to sit while a young man sketched her. After twenty minutes the picture was pretty but neither Alice nor Evie could recognize it as being a true likeness of Alice.

At eight that evening, dressed, and ready for Antoine's, a taxi took the girls from the side door of the hotel and left them at the restaurant. Seated at a table, the evening of culinary delights began. Alice had the game pate` and Evie the Escargot Bourguignon. Alice tasted one of Evie's snails in garlic and butter sauce and Evie said she liked the buttered toast that that held a portion of the pate'.

They both ordered the Filet with Marchand de Vin with a Chateauneuf du Pape wine and finished their meal with the Baked Alaska with chocolate sauce. Coffee and Napoleon Brandy ended the night. The taxi ride back to the hotel passed the big casino in town but the girls were both looking forward to a good night's sleep.

Early the next morning Evie and Alice left New Orleans to get back to university. The drive was long, but the music on the radio was good and stops to eat and refuel the car helped to get both of them back into the mindset to resume their studies. They knew this would be their last big vacation before graduation.

THE NOTE

Aunt Dorie was asleep in her recliner when Alice returned from her vacation. She unpacked and filled the laundry hamper with her beach outfits and a couple of things from the trip to New Orleans. A rustle in the pocket of her jeans she had worn at the beach caught her attention. She extracted the note from her pocket and then remembered she had been given the small envelop at the condo/hotel where she and Evie had stayed near the beach.

She turned the envelope over in her hand and decided now would probably be a good time to read it. The paper was a good quality stationary weight, much like the personal cards and envelopes her mother had used. The envelope was monogramed with a DAH. She didn't know anyone with those initials but tore open the note anyway. In a neat handwriting the note said:

Dear Miss Alice Blake:

I wish to thank you for your swift action when my mother Cora Khoury had difficulty breathing because a fish bone had lodged in her throat. My father and I will be eternally grateful since the incident could have had a more tragic outcome.

If you could please meet my father and I for lunch in the Coleman House Hotel at 11:00 this morning, we would like to thank you in person. Please bring your friend with you.

Best Regards,

Charles Alexander Khoury, M.D.
(555) 866-4881

Hm, Dr. Salek had warned her about a Dr. Khoury, she wondered if this was the Dr., she should be wary of or possibly it was a different one. Well, she would never know since the invitation was not acknowledged and she was no longer anywhere near the Coleman House Hotel. Alice threw the note on her desk and took her laundry basket to the basement.

Alice looked around her room. She usually tried to do a good cleaning of the room before she started each semester and had a couple of days to get it done but figured she would start in the afternoon. First, she needed to clear out the last course from her desk so the next one could begin to make stacks and piles of journal articles copied from the internet, library books, and the notes Alice always made in class. She was happy that her room had enough open bookcase space for her to put each course in. The graduate thesis would rely heavily on many of the things she had already studied and every research foray of the internet turned up at least one peer-reviewed journal article relating to her thesis topic.

Aunt Dorie woke up from her nap when Alice was in the kitchen making herself a sandwich for lunch. The old lady sat at the kitchen table while Alice worked. She put a portion of soup out for her aunt to eat for her lunch.

"How was your trip, dear?" her aunt said, "It seems you had some excitement. A young man has been calling here and left you some messages. He said he was coming this afternoon to thank you for saving his mother's life!"

Alice shook her head, "It wasn't that big a deal. When Evie and I were at the Surf Club a woman at the table next to us couldn't breathe and I tried helping her. We got her on the floor and I got a fishbone out of her throat that was choking her. EMTs came and took her away. Her husband thanked me and that was that."

"I'm sorry, Auntie, if this guy has bothered you. I just found the note he had left at the place Evie and I were staying at but I put it in my pocket and didn't read it until about an hour ago." Alice took her sandwich, cut it in half and gave her aunt the other half. She poured a glass of water for her and got an energy drink for herself.

Alice had been back to her task of sorting through the things she needed from her last class when she heard the doorbell. She heard her Aunt Dorie answer and invite someone in. A soft knock on her door prompted a reply. "Yes Aunt?"

Aunt Dorie opened the bedroom door and said, "There is a visitor here for you."

Alice was cleaning and organizing her room when she turned to see a tall man with dark hair standing in her room. "Hm, so you are Alice Blake. My father said you were a beautiful young woman." He put out his hand to shake Alice's. "My name is Dr. Khoury and I wanted to thank you for saving my mother's life at the Surf Club the other night."

Alice stood in front of her visitor. Her Aunt had retreated from the doorway and she was alone with a tall, good-looking man. "I apologize for not answering your note sooner, my friend Evie and I left for New Orleans and I put it in my pocket. I didn't find it until today."

"I expected that must have been the case. My father and I were sorry we missed you. Mother is fine and she and father are back home. I was supposed to be at that dinner but a, uh, patient needed me." Dr. Khoury was still holding Alice's hand and seemed reluctant to let it go.

He looked around the room at the clutter, totally different from the neat house he had walked through on the way to this girl's room Hm, he would never allow such slovenliness in his house.

"Your Aunt told me you were a student at the university. What are you studying?" he said.

Alice pulled her hand away and walked a few feet away from the Dr., "I'm doing my graduate work on the Middle Ages. It's fascinating to study and I'm one course and a thesis away from graduating. I'm glad your mother is doing better; I just did what I was trained to do when I was caring for my own mother."

"Your own mother?" Dr. Khoury asked. "And how is she doing?"

Alice looked down, "Dr. Khoury, my mother is dead, that is why I live with my aunt. As I said," she looked into his eyes, "I'm glad your mother is doing well. Let's leave it at that." She stood by the door. "Thank you for coming. You didn't have to, but I have some work to do. You can see yourself out."

He wasn't used to being dismissed in this way. He put his hand on the door about Alice's head. "Thank you for seeing me then. Can I take you to dinner? You have to eat you know and I still want to make up for the dinner which was interrupted at the Surf Club when Mother had her problem."

Alice's eyes bored into him, "Mister, oh, forgive me, Dr. Khoury, I'm fine, I didn't miss dinner, and I don't need any further thanking. Enjoy the rest of your afternoon, just let me get on with mine."

"Very well then. Enjoy your day." Dr. Khoury turned, walked through the living room and said goodbye to Alice's Aunt Dorie before showing himself out.

Alice resumed her cleaning and sorting but David Khoury hesitated at his car. He looked back at the little cottage. Hmm, little Alice was pretty, but a bit on the rude side. He had caught a whiff of her hair and smelled lavender. She had lovely hair and her skin was tanned but it suited her coloring. Interesting, he still wanted to take her out, but was it to thank her for his mother or for himself. He'd have to think on that.

Late the next afternoon Alice had finished her room and was ready to spend some time with Evie. They planned to meet at Shakespeare's that evening and then go on to Spider Joe's later. Alice wore a simple silk leopard print dress, Evie was in a slinky bronze shift and they both wore simple light jackets.

Albert Shakespeare was British and had been a professor at the university. He'd bemoaned the fact there wasn't a decent pub in the area and when he retired, he opened Shakespeare's. The walls were paneled in oak, the bar was divided into a main room and a smaller, private room, and the darts board had a prominent place near the bar. Most university kids were underage, but graduate and above found it a wonderful place to eat "pub grub" and discuss ideas and drink.

Alice and Evie were regular customers for the food and the occasional glass of beverage. The barkeep waved at them when they came in and found a seat. The waitress, Angie, was at the table with menus before they could sit down. The room was almost full but the table near them was still unoccupied.

The girls were about to leave when a man and woman sat down at the table next to them. The background music and chatter were enough to make the fact someone was sitting near them unremarkable.

"Good evening, Miss Blake," the man said. When Alice didn't respond or look in his direction, he repeated himself, only loud enough to cut through the noise. "Good evening, Miss Blake."

Alice looked at the man sitting at the table and realized it was Dr. Khoury. She nodded her acknowledgement of him and prepared to leave with Evie. Another look at the table and she saw a young woman, eyes lowered, sitting across from the doctor. Alice dropped the tip on the table and made her way through the crowd following her friend.

The night was getting chilly and both girls put on their jackets against the dropping temperatures. Alice felt a hand helping her with her hers and once it was settled about her shoulders, turned to see the doctor looking down at her.

A half smile crossed his lips. "Do you always dismiss people so easily. Usually when someone greets a person, the least that is expected is a verbal reply. Hm, maybe you don't think I deserve such a courtesy," he said.

Alice looked him in the eyes. "Sorry but we were about to leave, so hello doctor and goodbye. Have a nice evening." Alice turned and got into the cab Evie had hailed. The doctor was left standing on the street looking after a departing taxi. He did hear Alice's friend tell the driver to take them to Spider Joe's.

Spider Joe's was the local dance club used by some of the older university students and young professionals in the Green Valley/

Oakland area. Evie and Alice were regular visitors to the VIP area and was known to all the staff. Before the girls had removed their coats and sat on the couch, their favorite drinks were on the coffee table where they usually sat. They never had to stand in line to get in and, except on nights when they had classes the next morning or it was near the end of term when papers needed to be finished, they would stay until at least one in the morning.

The DJ at the club was an artist and moved the tunes along in an almost seamless wave of music that was pleasant to listen to and could be danced to quite easily. A man familiar to Evie began dancing with the girls and when a slower tune began, he took Evie in his arms and left Alice to sway to the familiar song.

Alice didn't mind dancing alone. She was an only child and when her friend wasn't visiting her, she often swayed to the beat of the music as she listened to songs in her room. Eyes closed; she didn't notice the figure of Dr. Khoury as he slipped his arm around her waist.

"I've finally got you Miss Blake," he whispered in her ear as he pulled her to him. "To busy to have dinner with me, but I see you have plenty of time for clubbing."

Alice's eyes flew open and she tried to pull away. "My family doctor warned me about you and told me to stay away. Now let me go this instant!" She was all but shouting over the music. Alice brought her right hand up in an attempt to slap the snarky smile off his face.

David Khoury was quicker than Alice and caught her hand before it could hit his cheek. "Violence Miss Blake? People don't hit me and a mere girl especially won't slap my face." With his arm around her waist and her right arm pulled around behind her, she was pressed up against his body. "Now, tell me about this family doctor who thinks he knows me, he breathed in her ear.

Alice turned her face up to him. "Uh, uh, he's an old family friend, Dr. Salek in Oakland." The closeness of her body to his was embarrassing. The short dress she was wearing was not made for such an embrace and Alice worried about what others might see of her body.

Just as suddenly as he had taken the liberty to pull her to him, he released her. "Salek, you say. Hm, I can understand why he might say that. Did he tell you why or was it just a blanket warning?"

Alice smoothed her dress and took a step back. "He just warned me to stay away from you."

David again took Alice's hand and before she could protest, was pulling her toward one of the private rooms that lined the back of the VIP area of the club. "Look little girl, before you paint me evil, let me tell you my side of why Salek is warning you against me." He pushed her onto one of the sofas in the room.

A waitress, seeing the couple enter the room, pulled back the drape to ask if they wanted drinks and with a growl, David sent her scurrying away. Standing before Alice, he began to talk.

"Dr. Salek has a daughter, she was in med school the same time as I was. We had a brief affair and then her father ended it. He had found a man that was wanting to marry her and he was appalled at our behavior. The man found out about the affair, that she was no longer a virgin, and refused to marry the girl. Salek blames me for ruining his daughter's life. End of story."

Alice could see the angry look in David's eyes. "Surely the girl had a name. Do you treat all of your 'conquests' as if they are nothing more than some generic object for your delight?"

The look he gave her had turned from anger at having to explain himself to indignation at the way Alice talked to him. For several long seconds she stared him down then got up to leave. "I think you have explained enough. If you had known, or cared to know anything about their culture, you might have had an understanding of why Dr. Salek would warn any woman against you. Good night, and don't come near me again."

David shot back, "you evidently don't know as much as you think you do little girl. My family comes from that same culture." Before he could react to her leaving, David saw Alice disappear through the curtains which separated this private space from the rest of the VIP area.

Evie and Alice walked out of the club and took a taxi to Evie's place. Alice took the cab on to her aunt's cottage. They both had one more free day before classes were to start.

School

several weeks had passed since the term break and the encounter with Dr. David Khoury was simply an unpleasant memory. Alice was swamped in her final class before having to start her graduate thesis. She always emersed herself in whatever she was studying and except for an occasional lunch with Evie, her time was spent either in class, the library, or in her room reading and composing her last term papers.

One of the only things Alice had kept of her father's was a 1968 Mustang Shelby. Her father had driven it when he was in college and he had kept it in pristine condition. Growing up, she had been told that when she went to college, it would be there for her to drive. After her father died, her mother had kept the servicing of the car with the same people to whom her husband had entrusted all of their cars. As Alice had to take over more and more of the responsibility for running the house where they both lived, the upkeep of the car was just another check she had to write each month.

As her mother's bouts with cancer became more debilitating, her father's college car took on less and less importance. Alice's days were filled with her schooling, overseeing the nurses who cared for her mother around the clock, and the hours of each day when she would sit and read to her mother. Her final responsibility was to plow through the years of memories attached to all of the things in the family home as it was stripped bare of furnishings and prepared for sale.

A storage facility near her old home was rented on a yearly basis and within its climate-controlled units she had stored those things she thought she might like to have in the future. The estate paid the rent and insurance on the three large storage units and except for an occasional memory of something specific, Alice rarely thought of the things.

The car, of course, did not go into storage but Alice used it when she wanted to go further than the short walk she usually had between her aunt's house and the school. Today was one of the days when she took the car for the drive over to Oakland.

The old family home had been sold a few months after her mother died and the money from the sale was added to the trust fund that her mother had established after her father died and the sale of his share of the company which his grandfather had founded, was added to the monies Alice would control in her inheritance on her twenty-fifth birthday. Her birthday was a few months away and the bank where the trust fund was managed asked for a meeting with her to discuss the handover.

The underground parking of the bank was convenient for the customers and Alice pulled into a slot near the elevator. The man she needed to see had offices on the seventh floor and she had been told, by his secretary, to come up directly from the carpark, thus avoiding the busy lobby. When the elevator stopped on the seventh floor, the doors opened to a plush carpet and a picture-perfect reception area with a slender, coiffed, and stylish receptionist. Alice gave the girl her name and was taken to the office of the man she was to meet.

Mr. Lawrence Jefferies had been a friend of her father when her dad was still alive and her mother had entrusted him with setting up and managing part of the trust fund she had opened for Alice. Lawrence came around from behind his desk and shook Alice's hand. "You are looking well. How is school going? You should be about to finish or are you going on for a Ph.D.?"

Alice smiled at the man. He was almost totally bald and a bit beefier than she remembered from her last visit to the bank after her mother died. "I'm doing fine. I don't think I'll go for the doctorate. That would be another six years and I'm about done with school." She took a seat at the conference table the man had led her to and looked at the pile of folders already stacked near the head of the table. "What do you need me for today?"

He took his seat where the folders were located and put on his 'serious banker face' for Alice. "You will be having a birthday soon and there are some of the investments that have various maturity dates attached to them. I just need to go over some of these with you so I know what you want done with them. Do you want to keep them as they are or cash out now and put the resultant funds in another investment vehicle?"

For the next two hours Alice waded through the various folders the banker had before him. Mr. Jefferies explained the pros and cons of making changes and what would happen if nothing was done. They had finally gotten down to the last folder. "This is a bit different. Uh, a few years before your dad passed away, he bought a piece of property. Nothing has been done to it and except for the estate paying the taxes on it each year, it simply sits there not making any money for your trust fund."

Alice looked at the deed in the folder. She read through the legal description of the property which didn't mean anything to her, but when she got to the part about the size, she was surprised to see it was more than fifteen acres. "Why would my dad have fifteen acres of land in, uh" she looked again at the deed, "Clearwater, wherever that is?"

Mr. Jefferies shook his head. "I don't know, but there was an inquiry about the property a few weeks ago. A real estate agent contacted the bank as financial agent for your trust fund. Somehow, they knew it was part of the estate of your late parents. A buyer seems interested but no further communication with the agent was forthcoming."

Alice looked at it again. "I guess just leave it. If someone was really wanting it, they would get back to you." She took a piece of note paper and jotted down the address. "Maybe I'll have a look at it someday." She pushed her chair back and stood to leave. "Thank you for your time, but I need to get back to my books."

Mr. Jefferies opened his office door and whished her a safe trip back to Green Valley. The drive back to Green Valley and her aunt's cottage was uneventful. She did call Evie and asked her if she wanted to have dinner with her. The two planned to meet at a nice little Italian place, Gino's, for some pasta and wine. She put her dad's Shelby back in the garage and the trip to Oakland was finished.

Evie was early to the restaurant and got a table near the back. She watched for Alice and was happy to see she had made it. Like herself, Alice usually lost upwards of five pounds each term because of lack of eating. When it came to their classwork, it took precedence over food. Good meals like the one they were about to have would just keep each of them from losing more weight. Vacation eating and drinking between terms usually brought them back to their normal weight.

The weather had started to turn warmer so Alice was only wearing a light jacket over her dress. When she came into Gino's, Evie could see her friend was probably the skinniest she had seen her since high school. The generous bust was still there and the curvy hips, but her legs were even more slender than she could ever remember. This girl needed a big plate of pasta more than she did!

Gino Rossi was in his late 60s and had worked his whole life here in America. Originally from Florence, he had migrated to the U.S. when he was fifteen. His wife, Luchella, had given him four sons and a beautiful daughter. The boys had all worked in the restaurant and his daughter had been a hostess until she married and moved to Miami with her husband. The boys all went to college and the hard work he and his family put into the restaurant had paid for all of it. Now he had grandsons working in the kitchen and a granddaughter who was hostess in place of his dearly departed Luchella.

Gino recognized the girls as repeat customers and he was the one who took their orders and brought them the bottle of wine. The blond was a good-looking girl, but a closer look at the brunette made him think of a picture he once saw in the Palazzo Pitti in his hometown of Florence. She had a beauty about her that radiated warmth like the painting of the Madonna he remembered. Hm, she would make him some beautiful grandchildren. Maybe his oldest grandson, Paulo, should be the one to bring their food from the kitchen? Gino headed through the doors of the kitchen to have a word with the boy.

Gino looked through the window of the kitchen door and was soon followed by a younger, very handsome young man. Paulo liked what he saw at table twelve, but really wished his grandpa would stop trying to fix him up with girls. However, he was a dutiful young Rossi and following his grandpa's lead he took the salads and breadsticks out to the table with the senior Rossi so he could be introduced.

Gino smiled at the two girls as he put the salads and breadsticks before them. "You see Paulo," he said turning to his grandson, "these lovely young ladies come often to eat here at Gino's." Motioning to Paulo, "this is my grandson, Paulo, Paulo Rossi. He is studying at the university to be a master of business, MBA."

Paulo shook Evie's hand as she said, "Evie Marsh and this is my friend Alice Blake. I'm working on my Master's in Latin and Alice is doing a Master's in the history of the Middle Ages."

"Wow," Paulo exclaimed as he shook hands with Alice. "Latin is not easy and neither was history, at least for me." He held onto Alice's hand just a bit longer than was normal, but he was looking into her eyes and didn't want to let go.

"Thank you, Paulo, but the course you are on is not easy either." Alice liked the handsome man who was smiling down at her. She really didn't mind that he was taking his time shaking her hand. "Perhaps we shall see you around campus someday."

Paulo smiled at Alice and commented, "I would look forward to that, but I must get back to the kitchen." Gino smiled at Evie and Alice before joining Paulo in the kitchen.

By the time the tiramisu was eaten and the coffees finished, Paulo had gotten both Evie and Alice's phone numbers. Alice called an Uber who took her home and then drove Evie to her lodgings. The usual mid-term dinner out would be the last until both had turned in their final papers. They did have plans for a 3-day vacation before the next term started, but this was not the time to think about that.

Alice did see Paulo twice for coffee on campus, but they both had heavy schedules plus the time he worked in his grandpa's restaurant, didn't really give them enough time to see each other. Paulo was graduating at the end of the term and Alice and Evie both received invitations to his party at Gino's the night of his graduation.

The Rossi family welcomed the two girls with open arms and the restaurant was closed that night for the private party. The food was great and the wine glasses were never empty. Alice and Evie had a great time, but they were driving up to a place upstate where they were going to spend their three days of relaxation before their thesis terms started. They left just after the graduation cake was cut.

Before leaving, Paulo and Alice had a quiet moment alone. "Alice, I want to see you when you get back from your trip. Grampa is already in love with you and I agree with him. Let me take you out, just the two of us. Don't you want to see where this could go? I know I do." Paulo squeezed her hand and kissed her on the forehead. "Please save some time for me."

Alice took her hand back and breathed, "I will think about you and let you know when we get back, okay?" Paulo stepped back and nodded. He opened the door to the Uber Evie had summoned and waited for the two girls to get in. Alice turned as the car drove off and saw Paulo, bathed in the glow of the streetlight, waving goodbye.

Early the next morning, Alice and Evie started the three-hour drive to the lake house where they would spend the next three days decompressing from the last term. Along the way, Alice told Evie about the private encounter with Paulo.

"Don't get me wrong, he's handsome and he's starting a great job in a month, but do you really like him?" Evie was doing what any good friend would, play devil's advocate. "His family is wonderful, and speaking as an only child like you, there are a lot of them! You know his whole crew would be watching you and everything you and Paulo did together."

Alice frowned. "I hadn't thought of that. I mean, he's not asking to marry me, just go on a date."

Evie laughed, "a date it may be to you and him, but his family, especially Gino, the granddad, is going to see it as the first step down the aisle. I mean, he's the one that fixed you up with him in the first place."

"Hm, I guess you're right. Maybe I shouldn't go out with him, but I am attracted to him." Alice needed to think a long time on getting any closer to Paulo. In her mind she was thinking, I wonder if he would let me call him Paul.

Evie watched her friend. She could see she was thinking about him. Time to get her back in the moment, "tell me about this lake house. I hope it's got all of the amenities. Are there any good restaurants nearby, or do you plan on cooking for us?"

She left her musings about Paulo and came back to the here and now. "Oh, yes, it's got all kinds of stuff around there, not far from the house. I'm sure some even deliver."

BACK TO THE BOOKS

The trip to the lake house had done both of them a world of good. Rested, refreshed, and ready to begin the final push toward their graduations, they parted on the Wednesday night ready to get to work. Alice had thought about Paulo a few times on the vacation, but hadn't yet come to an answer. Besides she was too tired to think about that as she pulled into her aunt's garage and put the Shelby away for the night.

Thursday morning, Alice started the end of term cleanup of all of the books and papers she had used in the semester just past. The trash was all put in bags, important papers put in the pile for her thesis, and any stray books were set aside to be returned. She looked over her room and was happy with the progress.

Shortly before five in the afternoon Paulo called. "Hi Alice, how was the trip?"

She frowned, she didn't expect he would be wanting to call her so soon, "it was nice. Evie and I just spent the time sleeping in, sunning on the dock, and eating way more than we should."

"Well, I hope you are hungry today because I'd like to take you to dinner. Oh, don't worry, I know a lot more places to eat besides grandpa's place. Fancy some steak or maybe Middle Eastern would suit you better," Paulo replied.

Alice made up her mind, "Middle Eastern sounds like fun. What time?"

She could almost hear Paulo smile when he replied, "Pick you up at seven?"

"Sounds fine," Alice said, "see you then. You have the address, right?"

"Absolutely!"

Paulo was at her aunt's front door at exactly seven. Alice told her Aunt Dorie goodnight and left on her date.

"Mm, you look wonderful tonight." Paulo looked closely at his date. The dress was short, but not too short and besides it showed off her long, shapely legs, her curvy hips, and oh her breasts, he could get lost in those.

He longed to see her naked under him as he prepared to see for himself if she was still untouched. Not many girls her age would not have had at least one or two relationships, including sexual partners that were not long-term. He'd even asked around among some of his classmates at the university and no one had known her to ever go out with anyone. Interesting, but how to find out without asking her directly? A challenge it was then, he was definitely up for it!

The Middle Eastern restaurant had valet parking and Paulo left the keys with the boy who would park it. Opening Alice's door, he offered her his hand for her to step out. He was being the perfect gentleman and would continue to be until it was time not to be.

Michell's was very busy. Paulo asked the host for a booth and was told it would be about a five-minute wait. "Would you and the young lady like to wait in the bar? I will come and get you when we are ready," said the tuxedo-clad maître d'.

Paulo took Alice's arm and found her a seat at the bar. He stood next to her and surveyed the other people in the room. No one looked like they might make any unwanted advances towards his date and he relaxed while they waited. No sooner had they ordered cocktails when the maître d' was ready to show them to a booth.

A waiter came with their drinks and they both perused the menus. Alice saw a lamb and okra stew with rice which looked interesting and Paulo asked her about sharing an appetizer of stuffed grape leaves or spinach and feta pastries with pine nuts. They agreed on the stuffed vine leaves and gave their order for the main course. The wine steward came and a light white wine was chosen to go with their meal.

"Paulo," Alice began, looking him straight on to gauge his reaction to her coming suggestion. "I was thinking about it at your graduation party the other night, but would you mind if I called you Paul? I mean I would understand if you didn't like that, but maybe it would be okay for me to do that." She lowered her gaze to toy with her drink glass.

He chuckled, "I have been trying to get someone to call me Paul since I was in grade school! Every year I would tell the teachers, mostly nuns in the school I went to, please call me Paul, but every time it was Paulo this and Paulo that. No, I don't mind at all sweet Alice," he reached out and touched her hand. "You can call me anything you want."

Out of the corner of her eye, a familiar figure was approaching the table. "Miss Blake, Miss Alice Blake, how nice of you to be here." Alex Khoury, the father of David Khoury got their attention.

Alice turned to talk to the gentleman, "It's good to see you again. I hope you wife is doing okay after the last time I saw you in a restaurant."

Paul looked at the man with a questioning frown. He knew Alex Khoury from his grandfather, Gino. The Khoury family owned several restaurants in this general area but he didn't know Alice was familiar with the head of the Khoury family.

Alex noticed the wariness of the young Rossi. "Miss Alice saved my wife's life a few months ago. We were eating in a restaurant on the Gulf when my Cora got a fish bone stuck in her throat and this girl was the one who saw my wife's distress and acted to remove the bone and begin CPR." Alex turned and signaled the maître d', "Joseph, this couple are my guests for the night."

Paul began to object, but Alex was adamant, "this is the least I can do to thank Miss Alice for what she did." He shook Paul's hand and patted Alice on the arm. "Enjoy your meal."

During the rest of the meal Paul began to get a better feeling for the young woman sitting before him. He knew she was pretty, no not pretty, that wasn't a strong enough word, mm, she was gorgeous. Not is a glamorous way like a Hollywood movie star, but she shown. She was also smart and the conversation with her showed she could also be funny. Alex Khoury already thought her some kind of hero, yep, this was probably the kind of girl you wanted to take home to mama.

The waiter had cleared away the last of the plates and another brought a coffee for each and brandy. "Alice," Paul began, "I'd like to take you out again very soon. I know you will be beginning your thesis courses soon, but do you think you can make some time for me?" He reached over to take her hand and found no resistance when she didn't pull hers away.

"I would like that but until I get things sorted with my thesis chair and the rest of the committee, I'm going to be very busy. I just don't know if I'll have the time or not. Can I let you know on this?" Alice had a good time and Paul was good looking and all, but did she want to continue seeing him? Maybe the fact she would be super busy these next few months while she was doing her graduate thesis were a chance to sort out how she really felt about him.

He squeezed her hand, "I understand. Let me take you home and maybe you can find some time for me. You can text me anytime and if you even have time for only a coffee, I will be happy to be with you." Paul got up and held Alice's chair. He took her hand as they thanked the maître d' and asked him to again convey their thanks to Alex Khoury for the wonderful meal.

Paul gave the valet the parking stub for his car and the boy left to get it. Alice shivered and Paul put his arm around her shoulder in an attempt to make her warm. A man came up behind them and pulled Paul's hand away angrily.

"Take your hands off of her!" David Khoury all but screamed at Paul Rossi. "Don't you ever let me catch you pawing this girl again!"

"Doctor Khoury, how dare you behave that way!" Alice icily confronted David Khoury. "What gives you the right to talk to Paul that way?"

Paul stood between David and Alice, "what do you think you're playing at Khoury, she is my date and you come along and spoil it for us. Go home and grow up. Get your own girl!"

The valet had the car at the curb and the passenger door open. Alice slid into the seat and Paul closed the door. Before he walked around to the driver's side, he had one last jab to take at David. "She's mine, and don't you forget it!"

Seething, David retorted, "We'll see about that!" he exclaimed as the car's taillights disappeared around the corner. Hmph, yes, we shall see which one of us gets to little Alice first, Mr. Paulo Rossi!

The first meeting with Dr. Fisher, her thesis chair, was held in his office on campus. Alice had been in contact with him since he was chosen by her advisor in the middle of last term but the substance of their notes to each other so far had been no more than a get-to-know-you type of correspondence. Their face-to-face meeting was more specific.

"So, this will give you the guidelines I like to follow," the elderly professor said, handing a sheaf of papers to Alice. "I think you are on the right track with your thesis so far. I like your topic and I think you probably have enough material to start your work. I have always found that as a student progresses in their work, new material can lead to more material being added or things we thought we would need is discarded as irrelevant to the topic."

Alice looked at the papers she had been given. "Sir, according to your timeline, you want a minimum of one weekly update and a meeting every two weeks. If I should need more contact, will that be acceptable to you?"

Professor Fisher smiled, "Miss Blake, I would not only find that acceptable, but admirable. It is much easier to fix a problem before it happens or gets too big. You do understand that, right?"

Alice nodded, "Yes, professor, I'm thinking that might be good."

"Excellent, excellent," he said as he stood to signify the meeting was over. He went to the door of his office and held it open for Alice. "I will get back to you in a day or two about the rest of the members on your committee. Work on that outline and thesis statement and question. If you can get me a good statement and thesis question by the end of next week, I will consider you having gotten off to a good start. Enjoy the rest of your day." He closed his door as he watched Alice depart down the hall.

Alice was happy with professor Fisher. She had been told by others who had either taken classes from him or had him as a thesis advisor that he was an expert on the time about which she would be writing her thesis. She wanted that kind of knowledge to help her if she might stumble in preparing her work. Alice was also happy that, except for the required meetings and the odd trip to the library, she would be able to work from her aunt's house.

She was walking home from her meeting with the professor but was lost in thought. Alice didn't notice there was a car parked on the street in from her aunt's cottage until she heard a car door close and looking up, she saw David Khoury. She stopped to see what he would do.

"If you have come here to continue your bullying, go away. In fact, why are you here, are you stalking me?" Alice said acidly.

David held up both hands, "see, I'm perfectly harmless. It was just a shock seeing that boy with his arm around you."

"And why should that be any of your business? Last I looked we didn't know each other and I certainly haven't given you any rights over who I see or where I go." David had moved between Alice and the front door of her aunt's house.

"Look, you're a beautiful, vulnerable young lady and I just wanted to protect you." David said as he stood with his hands crossed before him.

Alice stared at him. "And who is going to protect me from you? Not that I need looking after, but perhaps I should ask Paul to protect me from your stalking."

David moved a bit closer, "so, it's Paul now. Hm, he always did want to be called Paul, he hated the Italian name he had been given." He noticed the look of surprise on Alice's face. "Oh, didn't he tell you? Humph, I've known him since he was a kid. He went out with a cousin of mine when he was in high school, took her to the Senior Prom he did. Not a very good dancer as I remember. Her parents thought he was cute, but she went away to college and married a lawyer."

"Well, doctor, all of that is very nice, but if you don't mind, I've got work to do and this briefcase is getting heavy. Enjoy the rest of your evening." She turned and stated to pass him to get to the door. David stepped out of the way but then asked her to have dinner with him.

"Look, I don't even like you so just leave me alone. Go pick on somebody else." She started to step up onto the front porch when he reached out for her.

David stood close to her and whispered in her ear, "I like you little Alice and someday we will be together. It will be me who takes you to places of ecstasy you have never known before, and it will be me who makes you understand what a truly sensual animal you can be."

Her eyes widened, the color drained from her face, before she turned a bright red. Alice looked at David as if a monster had taken his form. Her voice was quivering with rage, "Don't ever speak to me again or I shall call the police." Her key opened the front door and as she slammed it shut, she could hear David Khoury's laugh.

Over the next several weeks she had several calls from Paul. He told her about his new job and she let him know of some of her progress. Mostly, however, it was simply checking in with each other. She did get away for a coffee one Saturday afternoon after she had spent the morning in the library doing some research with Paul, but except for a sandwich with Evie one Monday, Alice had been at home, hard at work.

During one of the long phone calls Alice had with Evie, she had told her friend about the encounter she and Paul had with David Khoury at his dad's restaurant and the episode outside of her aunt's house the day she had first met her thesis chair. She didn't tell Evie what he had said, that was still something she was having trouble with herself. Thankfully she hadn't seen David since.

Alice was sitting in her room immersed in her work when she heard a loud bang followed by a scream. She pushed her desk chair back so fast it collided with the bed. Alice could hear pained cries from the kitchen.

She didn't like what she saw when opening the kitchen door. Her aunt was on the floor with a knife in her hand. There was some blood, but her aunt was whimpering and making no effort to get up. Alice knelt beside her. "Aunt Dorie, Aunt Dorie," her aunt neither looked at her nor acknowledged her. Alice saw the knife was responsible for a small cut on the opposite hand and Alice took it from her aunt.

She pulled her cell phone from her pocket and called 911. An ambulance was on its way. Alice took a shawl from the couch and covered her aunt with it to keep her warm while the EMTs came to her aid. Alice unlocked the from door and got the list of her aunt's medication from off of the fridge door. She also got her aunt's purse in case they needed the insurance information.

Alice stroked her aunt's brow and held her hand while she waited for the ambulance. She heard the siren and when the knock came on the front door, she called out for them to come in. "We're in the kitchen! It's my aunt, she fell and is not looking very good."

The emergency service went to work on her aunt and they put her on a gurney to transport her to the hospital. Alice got her bag and her aunt's purse before going to the garage to get the Shelby. She also got a jacket and her laptop in case she would have to stay with her aunt for a long time.

She pulled into the emergency room parking lot shortly after her aunt was taken inside. While the nurses had her aunt in an exam room where they were taking her vitals, starting an IV, and beginning an EKG, Alice was giving her aunt's insurance information to the hospital's bean-counters.

Alice tried to get some information on her aunt when she had finished signing her in for treatment, but was told she would have to wait in the ER waiting room. Several minutes later, a nurse came out to ask Alice to accompany her to her aunt's room.

Never had Alice seen her aunt look so helpless. She was surrounded by machines, a couple IV bags were hanging from the head of her bed, and a monitor was taking her blood-pressure every few minutes. Her aunt's eyes were closed and she was pale.

"What happened?" was Alice's first question but before she could go on, the nurse cut in.

"We are trying to pin that down right now. I have a few questions for you first." Alice nodded at the nurse. "I need you to tell me what happened."

Alice took a deep breath. "I was in my room, studying, and I heard a crash and a scream. When I went into the kitchen, I saw her laying on the floor with a knife in her hand. There was blood and at first, I thought she had somehow stabbed herself, but when I went to her side, it was just blood from where she had cut her hand. I called 911 for the ambulance, next I unlocked the front door so the EMTs could get in and I found the list of medications she takes. After a few minutes the first responders came and began working on her."

"Mm huh, did you move her at all or try to give her mouth to mouth?" the nurse asked.

"No, she was breathing and I didn't move her. I don't know what happened to her, she was just on the floor like she had collapsed or something." Alice just wanted to know her aunt's condition and couldn't understand all of the questions.

"Okay, that tracks with what we have found. Your aunt has a heart condition and she seems to have suffered a stroke. The ER doctor has called in a couple of specialists to go over her test results. They are doing that right now. As soon as there is any news, I will let you know." The nurse check one last reading on the machine doing periodic EKG's and left the room.

A chair beside her aunt's bed looked like the best place to wait. She reached out for her aunt's hand and found it a bit cold. With her other hand, she pulled out her phone to send a text to Evie and she also sent a text to the professor to let him know the zoom meeting they had planned would have to be delayed and the reason for the delay.

Less than a half hour later, Evie was at her side. The two talked in hushed tones not to disturb Alice's aunt. The nurse who had been in before came back to check the heart monitor and the amount of solution that was in one of the IV drip bags.

"When will my aunt wake up?" Alice said in a hushed voice. "She looks like she is just sleeping but is that what it is, sleeping, or something else?"

"Miss Blake, when the doctors come to talk to you, they will explain everything. It shouldn't be too much longer." As if on cue, two men in white coats came into the room.

The older of the two said, "Miss Blake, I'm doctor Hall and this is doctor Diaz. I'm a cardiologist and doctor Diaz is a neurologist. We've done some scans and test on you aunt and it seems she had a stroke, but she also has a heart condition. We have given her something that we are hoping will alleviate the problem with the stroke, but the heart is worrying. She needs surgery and my colleague and I think she should be monitored for the next several hours to see if the medicine is effective before putting her through surgery."

Evie held Alice's hand as Alice spoke to the doctors. "Why isn't she awake?"

Dr. Diaz looked at one of the small bags hanging from the IV tree. "We thought it best to put her in a twilight sleep. It's not as deep as a coma, but it allows her body to rest and hopefully, begin to heal. We want to see if the effects of the stroke on her brain is lessened before we put her through an hours long heart surgery." He looked at Alice, "it was not what we would classify as a massive stroke, but neither was it some minor incident. There will be damage, we just want to try and keep it at a minimum."

The two men prepared to leave, before they went, Dr. Hall turned. "I'm having a heart surgeon, the best available man, come in to see your aunt's scans and test results. When it is determined she is well enough for the heart surgery, he will be doing it for her. There will also be a few more scans this afternoon and into the night. We want to monitor her condition and give the surgeon the best information to go on." With that, the two left.

Evie stayed with Alice for another couple of hours but as the day wore on, Alice sent Evie back to her work on the thesis she was writing for her Master's in Latin. Alice did ask Evie to bring her a couple of things in case she stayed with her aunt through the night.

Not long after Evie left, Alice received a text message from her professor telling her to contact him when they could reschedule the zoom meeting and he also said for her not to worry if it took a few days. "Take care of your aunt and yourself," was the last thing he wrote.

The nurse came in to tell her she could request a cot be put in the room if she wanted to stay with her aunt. "Since she is not going to be eating her dinner, you might as well eat it or you can go to the cafeteria. We also have a sandwich shop on the campus, but it's a bit pricy and over near the medical center offices. Take your pick but don't forget to eat."

Sitting with her aunt brought back memories of the long hours, days, and months Alice had sat at the bedside of her mother. Except for the last few months, her mother was lucid and talkative. Pain and the morphine used to control it was what robbed her mom of her faculties which was a shame because her mother had always been a great conversationalist.

Alice laid her head down on the bed as she held her aunt's hand. She was sure she had only closed her eyes for a minute, but a gentl hand was nudging her awake. Alice opened her eyes to see the darkness outside of her aunt's room window.

A soft male voice was calling to her, "Alice, Alice, it's time to wake up little Alice."

The 'little Alice' rang alarm bells. All vestiges of sleep were gone and she was fully awake. She stood and was looking into the eyes of David Khoury. "What, uh what are you doing here?" She was appalled this man had followed her to her aunt's sick room and she was so mad she was shaking. "Get out, go on, get out now!"

David stood with his arms crossed over his chest. His white doctor's coat was stiffly starched and almost rustled as he moved. "What I'm doing here is consulting on your aunt's condition and trying to determine when or if she should have heart surgery. Now if you will kindly calm down, I'll try to tell you how your aunt is and what I can do for her."

The mention of her aunt helped to calm her. "Dr. Hall is her cardiologist, why would he want you here?" Although spoken in low voices, the venom was still evident in her tone.

"Dr. Hall does not do heart surgery any longer and I do. I'm one of the best there is and the best in this area. If you doubt my credentials, we can go to my office over in the medical center and you can check out my diplomas. Now, do you want to know about your aunt or should I get another doctor to come and see her?"

Alice backed down and knew she needed to put her personal feelings aside in favor of her aunt's health. "Okay, a truce then, but don't think I've forgiven you for what you said."

"Fine, a truce it is. Now could you please sit down so we can discuss your aunt?" David held the back of the chair near Aunt Dorie's bed and when Alice was seated, he pulled another chair up beside her so they could talk about the medical crisis which had brought Alice's aunt to this specific problem and what possible measures could be taken to help the problem.

Alice held her aunt's hand while David told her about the history of the condition of her aunt's heart. "Your aunt was told, on more than one occasion, by Dr. Hall, that she needed surgery going back for more than two years. I've seen her records and it is clear than instead of resolving itself as your aunt thought it would, the problems only got worse. Yesterday, her condition degenerated when she had a stroke."

David went on, "the stroke was not as bad as it could have been, but coupled with the heart condition, it might have been deadly" an alarm on one of the machines in Aunt Dorie's room began sounding followed by another one which sounded like a claxon. David pulled Alice out of her chair and began walking her to the door. Nurses and another doctor rushed past her to get into the room.

David said in a commanding voice, "go sit out here and I'll come and get you once we get her stabilized." Alice started to object but he turned her to face him, "for once little Alice, do what you're told." He turned and disappeared into the room and closed the door.

Alice sat on one of the sofas in the Cardiac ICU waiting room. It was empty except for some chairs, a couple of tables, and a coffee bar with an empty coffee pot. She sat where she could see the door to her aunt's room and waited for news. A couple of doctors went in and out, but David was not one of them.

She was so engrossed with worry over her aunt she didn't see Paul walking down the hall towards her. He sat beside her on the couch and put his arm around her shoulders. "Why didn't you tell me about your aunt? I would have been here before but I had to hear about it from a cousin of mine in the ER."

Alice simply looked up at him, "I really only told Evie and my thesis chair about this."

Paul pulled her closer. She felt a certain comfort having someone with her during the wait for news. She put her head on his shoulder and kept watch on the door. A few minutes passed and a nurse came out of the door and headed toward where Alice was sitting.

Alice stood up and took a step toward the nurse. "Tell me, please, how is my aunt."

"I take it you are Alice Blake?" Alice nodded assent. "Dr. Khoury will be right out to talk to you but we need your signature on this consent form so he can do surgery on her." The nurse handed Alice a clipboard and started explaining what was needed. "Sign here, initial here, and print your name and your aunt's name here. Sign the last page and we can take her down to surgery."

Alice stood with a pen and did as she had been instructed. "When will David, uh Dr. Khoury be out to see me?"

"He should be out any minute. I need to take these forms to the desk," she turned and began walking to the nurse's station. The door to Aunt Dorie's room opened and two other doctors came out followed by David who headed over to where Alice was standing.

Half-way to where she was standing, the light above the door on her aunt's room began flashing and the claxon again went off. The doctor turned and rushed back into the room, closing the door. The nurse who had taken the papers from Alice followed soon after.

Paul stood with Alice. He put his arm around her waist and she leaned up against him. He looked down at her and a slight smile crossed his face. Alice was vulnerable right now and that might be to his advantage. She needed someone strong to lean on and it wasn't much further from comforter to maybe a little more. He had been wanting to get her alone and dependent on him and what better way than to be there for her during this trying time?

The door opened and some of the people started to leave. Alice started to walk to the door when David came out, his head down. When he looked up, he saw Alice but hadn't yet seen Paul. "Alice, I'm so sorry. We did everything we could but we couldn't even get her into surgery where we might have been able to save her."

Hearing what David had to say she stopped and stared at him. "But, but, I just signed the papers, what happened?" Paul moved to stand with her.

David finally saw Paul and his demeaner changed. "I didn't know you called this guy in."

Paul stepped toward David. "She didn't call me, I found out from a relative who works here that my girlfriend's aunt was admitted. I came as soon as I heard."

Alice turned, "girlfriend, girlfriend, nobody said anything about girlfriend, especially me. Now could you two infants stop your pissing contest long enough for me to find out what happened to my Aunt Dorie?"

David took Alice's hand and led her to one of the chairs in the waiting area. "Let's sit here so I can talk to you. Uh, there will be an autopsy, but I think what I am going to tell you will be what the findings of it will show." David took both of Alice's hands and looked her in the eyes. "Your Aunt Dorie has been suffering from heart disease for the last few years. The stroke she suffered yesterday afternoon was not a massive stroke, but it was big enough that one of the blood vessels that goes into the heart was put under pressure. You see, her veins were filled with plaque and the surgery she should have a two years ago would have alleviated that problem."

He went on, "the reduced blood flow to the heart over the years had weakened the heart muscle and this is why she was on so many medications. One of those meds was a blood-thinner that should have made it easier for her blood to flow through the narrowed veins. When she had the stroke, which was at a place in the brain where a vein had thinned out, bulged, and then ruptured, the thinner she was on created a bleed. I think it is this bleed that caused her death."

David watched Alice as she took in all of the information he was giving her and began to come to terms with the loss of her aunt. He had read the aunt's file and talked to doctors Hall and Diaz about the family history. With the death of her aunt, for all intents and purposes, Alice was now alone in the world with no living relatives.

There was Paulo Rossi hanging around in the background, but he was no match. No, little Alice would need a shoulder to cry on and he preferred it was his.

A commotion in the hallway disturbed his thought and Alice's friend, Evie, sat in the chair on the opposite side of Alice. "Oh Alice, I am so sorry about your Aunt Dorie, I just heard." Evie had her arms around her friend and Alice had her head on her friend's shoulder. Evie looked over at David and her expression was not kind.

David patted Alice on the arm and got up to leave. "I think you can go in now and sit with your aunt for a few minutes if you want to. The staff have probably had time to make her look comfortable. I suppose you can wait until tomorrow to begin making arrangements for her. The hospital will tell the funeral home when they will release her body."

For the first time, Alice looked at David with something other than contempt. "Thank you," was all she said.

Alice and Evie went into the aunts' room and closed the door. David turned to address Paulo. "Leave her alone Rossi, the girl has had a shock and she has her friend with her now to help her. Give her time to mourn and make arrangements for her aunt. It's the least you can do."

David disappeared through the door to the cardiac ICU suite. Paulo stayed for another few minutes but when Alice and her friend didn't come out, he decided he should leave and let Alice have her friend take her home.

Aunt Dorie's little bungalow seemed empty to Alice. She had lived with her aunt since selling the family home after her mother died and now, she was going to be doing the same with her last relative's place. The lawyer who handled her aunt's affairs sent Alice a copy of the will a few days after the funeral.

Everything her Aunt Dorie had owned she had given to Alice. This small house was close to the university and she could walk to her thesis chair's office and the library in a few minutes. The car had a garage and if she moved into an apartment, there may be no place to put the car. No, Alice decided to stay where she was until she at least finished her thesis and got her Master's degree.

Financially her aunt had given her a considerable sum. It was nothing like the amount she would have control over once she became twenty-five, but it gave her plenty of funds so she wouldn't have to tap her parent's estate for anything.

Both David and Paul had come to the funeral and the reception which followed. The little church where her aunt was a member did a lovely service and the ladies club hosted the reception which followed with finger-foods, and punch. After the reception, Alice and Evie returned to the cottage to share a bottle or two of wine.

While she was with Evie, she told her friend about the property her father had bought in a place called Clearwater. Alice had the idea that she might like to go see it on the weekend, if she had gotten her work on her thesis caught up, and wondered if Evie would go with her.

"Sure, and you don't know anything more than an address on this thing" Evie asked.

"Nothing, maybe we can take a picnic. If nothing else there is a nature reserve which borders the property on two sides. It might be nice to sit on the grass and have some lunch." She kind of liked the idea and said, "in fact, I'll pack the picnic basket myself." Alice was glad she had thought of the idea. She had more than her fair share of dead and dying and wanted to clear it from her head.

"My thesis chair has given me some things to do, but I'll have that all in order by the weekend so let's go." Evie thought it was just what Alice needed.

Alice's phone acted as the GPS and the girls found the property with no problem. A small lane which branched off of the main road was overgrown as was the property itself. The trees and brush were thick, but Alice turned the Shelby into the lane. She drove slowly, Alice worried she might get stuck and didn't want to have to back her car out onto the main road. A slight bend in the lane ahead and the thick foliage which had screened the property began to thin out. The lane continued on through a field of wildflowers, some of which were in bloom and others which had turned into brown stalks. The lane ended near a small lake.

"Gee, Alice, this is a surprise. When you really look at it, it's quite a nice piece of land. A bit remote for my tastes, but a really nice place." Evie liked the lake and the field of wildflowers the best. "What would you do with it though?"

Alice looked around as she got out of the car. There was a dock on the lake and it looked sturdy enough they might want to sit there to have their picnic. Evie started to get the things from the trunk, but a yelp from Alice got her attention. "Damn mosquitos! We can't get anywhere near this lake without being eaten alive!" She exclaimed.

Evie put the items back in the trunk. Alice backed the car up and turned around. She slowly moved the car about a hundred yards from the lake. If she wasn't close to water or heavy foliage, maybe the mosquitos wouldn't bother them. She was right and the girls found a place to spread the blanked, put the two folding chairs, and begin their picnic.

"I think you are right, this place is remote, but it's nice. I don't know why Dad bought it, but he must have wanted it for something." Alice sat so she could see the majority of the land she was supposed to own. "Maybe he wanted to build out here, but we had a perfectly good house in Oakland, way here?"

Evie shook her head, "It's nice, but too cutoff from everything. Oakland is a better place to live." She took another chicken salad sandwich. "Have you thought about what you will do after you finish your degree and sell your aunt's house?"

Hmm, that was a question Alice had been asking herself. She really had no plans for anything beyond getting her Master's degree. She could teach in a high school or even a community college, but that wasn't something that really suited her. Teaching in a university would necessitate her getting a Ph.D., but that was also another six years of study even if she was accepted into a doctoral program. No, it was more about having the degree her parents had wanted for her than anything else.

Alice would be twenty-five before the end of the semester and then she could inherit the estate her parents had left. The land they were picnicking on was a small part of what she assumed would be in the final tally of assets. She had to remember she had another meeting with the banker the day before her birthday.

"Honestly," Alice said, "I haven't any idea of what I plan on doing beyond my master's. What about you, are you still planning on an extended stay in Florence, Italy when you finish your Latin degree?"

Evie laughed, "My extended stay as you put it will be a two-year study tour with the emphasis on study and not much 'tour'." My dad still can't get his head around the money it will cost. He grips about everything from the amount I have to pay for the apartment I will share with three other students to the 'recommended' daily allowance for food and incidentals. I think he thought once the Master's was finished the costs would go down but if I want to get into any good doctoral program, I'm going to need a leg up and this next two years in Italy should do it!"

"Well, just don't go over there and snag some great looking Italian guy for a husband. I just don't know what I will do without you here and adding the extra impediment of being some guy's wife doesn't sound very good." Alice and Evie started to put the picnic things in the car for the trip back to the university and the cottage where Alice now lived on her own.

The final push to the end of the semester kept Evie and Alice busy. Any requests from Paul for coffee or a meal had to be declined and a very nice condolence card from David was appreciated.

Neither girl was going to take any time off between the semesters as they had throughout their undergraduate and now their graduate education. Both had revisions and rewrites to do and they needed to keep the momentum going to finish by the end of the spring semester.

Alice had dropped almost ten pounds since the semester started. Living alone in her aunt's cottage meant she didn't have to stop her work to ask Aunt Dorie if Alice could make her a sandwich or if her aunt wanted something from take-out. Coffee, a cup of soup, and tea kept Alice going.

Time, however, was fast moving towards Alice's twenty-fifth birthday and the day when she would need to take control of her own affairs. The will her father had the lawyers write up for him and his wife had the twenty-five-year clause as part of a protection for Alice not to be descended upon by male gold-diggers or fortune hunters. Neither of the two parents had expected to die as young or as soon as they had. The bank where her father had entrusted his estate was the same one used by Alice's mother when she died. The day before the birthday, Alice had an appointment with the banker to finish the paperwork which would make her the sole owner of her mother and father's combined estates.

Mr. Jefferies had asked Alice to make it a lunch meeting. She took the Shelby, parked in the underground garage of the bank, and made her way to the seventh-floor conference room. The receptionist seated Alice at the long table and left the room.

"Miss Blake, it is so good to see you again," the banker said in a cheery voice as he entered the room. "So, tomorrow is your twenty-fifth birthday and the day you will take over your parent's estate." He put the armload of papers and folders on the table and sat down.

Alice half smiled and ask him to please try to expedite the process. "I'm doing what I hope will be the last edits on my Master's thesis so I can graduate soon. I need to get back to my work."

Mr. Jefferies nodded. He placed one paper, folder, or sheaf of papers after another in front of Alice and indicated where she needed to sign. When it was done Alice was shaking her wrist and flexing her fingers. "Whew, I don't think I've ever had to sign so many papers at one time in my life. I hope this is the last of them."

Mr. Jefferies smiled and motioned for his secretary to come in and collect the signed papers. "I will have Wanda, my secretary, make copies of the ones you need, send the deeds you signed to the proper county clerks they can be registered, along with the fees, and by the end of our lunch you will have everything ready to take with you." He pulled a debit card from his jacket pocket. "This will give you ATM access to the savings and checking accounts after mid-night tonight. Call the number on the front tomorrow to activate it and set your unique pin."

The receptionist entered the room with a table service for Alice and Mr. Jefferies. She placed the salads down next and filled the water glasses. She had also put wine glasses on the table but when she tried to put wine in Alice's goblet, she declined. "I'm driving back to Green Valley and I still have a lot of work to do. I'll pass on the wine, but the salad looks great. Thank you!"

Back in her car twenty-minutes later, Alice put the debit card in her purse and began the drive back to the cottage. Professor Fisher, her thesis chair, had sent her some notes on the revisions she had done over the weekend of the last chapter of her thesis and she wanted to try and get the changes done before her birthday. She and Evie were in the homestretch of their respective degrees and tomorrow, Saturday, she wanted to celebrate knowing she was almost finished with her final paper.

After parking the Shelby in the garage, she next took the letters and such from the old mailbox attached to the cottage near the front door. Her aunt still received mail but it was mostly advertisements or catalogues with everything from gutter filters to cat themed pillows. A couple letters were for Alice and two birthday cards were also in the mail. She opened the letters and left the cards for the next day.

Alice's cellphone rang just as she got into the house. It was Paul, but did she want to talk to him right now? Might as well, "Hi Paul, what can I do for you."

"Well, the first thing you can do is tell me you'll let me take you out for a proper birthday dinner. Didn't you get my card?" Paul said.

Alice noticed one of the cards did have Paul's name in the return address. "Yes, I just got your card today, but my birthday is not until tomorrow and I never open my cards early. Besides, I'm working on the thesis, doing some, hopefully, final revisions." She reached down and opened the card.

Paul heard the tearing of paper and surmised, correctly it was Alice opening the card. "Well?" he said the anticipation. "Will you go out with me?"

She read the card and laughed at the cute design. "It's a wonderful card, thank you, but I still have the thesis to finish." She could almost hear his disappointment. "I tell you what, let me get this done and whatever day I turn in my finished thesis, we can go out. How does that work for you?"

"So," Paul said, "no matter when you finish, tomorrow, next week, or the week after, you will be happy celebrating your birthday with me then?"

"Paul, I promise. That is the best I can do, but the sooner I get off the phone, the sooner I can finish." Alice told him good bye and got back to work.

It was almost two am when she finished, but another read-through of the final chapter was a testament to her that she had done everything her professor had wanted. She knew that there was more she could have done and if she had wanted to continue on to a doctoral degree, this thesis was a good, strong start. She was, however, exhausted from this and wanted nothing more than to sleep. Before slipping into bed, she sent a copy of the finished thesis to her chair, Dr. Fisher, and the reader he had assigned her. If all went well, she would know by Monday if it was accepted.

Alice was bolted from her sleep by the persistent banging on the cottage door. She slipped a robe over her sleep-shirt and padded to the door. A delivery boy was standing behind a large bouquet of beautiful roses. From behind the blooms a teenage boy's voice said, "Are you Alice Blake?"

She laughed, "yes, I guess I am."

"Here, and sign this." The boy thrust the roses at her and followed it by a clipboard he had attached to his hip. "You have to sign for it, please."

Alice took the flowers, signed for the boy, and closed the door. The bouquet had a card, but putting them in water had to come first. She found one of the vases her aunt had in the kitchen and after putting the blooms in she went back to bed to finish her sleep.

The next interruption came from another delivery man who had two bunches of flowers and a wrapped package. The flowers were already in vases and she thanked the man and again tried to get some sleep. She settled into her bed, pulled the covers over her head, and disappeared into a dreamless date with Morpheus.

The phone and doorbell rang at about the same time. Alice emerged from her cocoon and checked the phone. It was Evie so she answered. "Hi, let me get the door and I'll call you right back." Before Evie could reply she had hung up the phone. The doorbell was also being used to excess and after putting a robe on she would deal with that.

This time it wasn't a delivery man but a large bouquet of lovely flowers had a man in a suit hidden behind it. "Look, just give me the damn flowers and let me get some sleep! Jeez, it's Saturday and I want a few extra hours of sleep!"

A laugh came from behind the flowers, "well happy birthday to you little Alice. Is this how you always greet people at your door?" David Khoury emerged from behind the foliage.

Alice froze when she heard his voice. She pulled her robe tightly around herself and blushed. "What are you doing here?"

David was smiling, "As I said, "Happy Birthday". I wanted you to have some flowers to brighten your day and thought I would bring them by myself. I hadn't seen you since your aunt's funeral and reception." He looked her up and down with a searing gaze. "I thought I would see how you were doing but I can see you have lost weight and are probably not eating well."

"I'm okay. I always lose some weight when I am working on my studies." She felt uncomfortable under his stare. "Uh, anyway, thank you for the flowers and the uh wishes." How to get him out of the cottage. "Look, I'm just getting up and need to get dressed. I hate to be rude, but can you go now?"

"Well," he said, "I could hang around and help, but sure, under one condition, have dinner with me."

"Oh, oh no I can't do that. I've already put Paul off until after my thesis is accepted so there is no way I'm going out with you." She started backing away. "Besides, I don't even like you!"

David crossed the space between them and had Alice's back to the wall. He put a hand on each side of her and leaned in. "Paul is not the boy for you. A man is what you need and I'm that man. Now when you understand this, it will make life easier on you." He didn't touch her but she could feel his breath on her cheek. He whispered in her ear, "I will be back little Alice and I will possess you. Believe this, dream about this, count on this."

She heard the door close and, in the distance, she heard a car pull away from the cottage. He was gone but his fragrance was still in her nostrils and his words in her ears. Alice stood against the wall as if impaled by his presence. Finally, she shook her head to clear her thoughts. A new sensation had befallen her, his words had made her squirm and she was wet. She sank to her knees.

The phone in the pocket of her robe pushed her back into reality. It took a bit to register and when she realized what it was, she fished it out and saw that Evie was calling her back.

"Hey girl, did you get lost or just forget about me and go back to sleep?" Evie said in a cheery, optimistic voice. "Worked late, huh? I had to finally quit around midnight before my brain just totally gave out on me. How much did you get done?"

Alice began to speak but the words didn't come, "Um, um," she coughed. "Minute" Alice went to the kitchen and got a bottle of water from the fridge. A big swig of the cold water helped to bring her back to her senses. "Oh, gee. It has been a morning. Deliveries and stuff, hard to sleep in when people need you to sign for stuff." She wasn't ready to tell her about David, she didn't even know about David.

"Oh, hey, I get it. So Happy Birthday anyway. Are we still doing some dinner out and a trip to the club?" Evie could tell her friend was in need of a little slack. "Why don't you call me when you get everything sorted out on your end?" The line went dead.

Alice stood in the middle of the small cottage kitchen looking at her phone. The visit from David had totally discombobulated her and she needed to get her bearings back. A shower should do it.

She sat at the vanity in her bedroom and combed out her long hair. Alice liked her long hair but it did need a trim. Maybe she could get it done sometime in the next week. The silence of the cottage was broken when an alert sounded on her laptop to tell her she had new emails. Hm, who could that be on a Saturday she thought?

Professor Fisher was sending her birthday wishes and congratulations on her final draft! This was something to celebrate! He also added a time when she would need to be in room 412 to defend her thesis before the full committee. Finally, the end was insight and the long hours of work, study, writing, and rewriting were almost over. She felt like a weight had been removed from her. She hadn't felt like this in a long, long time. Tonight, she and Evie really would celebrate!

Alice remembered the debit card the banker had given her and she pulled it from her purse, followed the directions on the sticky label on the front, and activated the card. While she sat at her computer, she accessed her personal bank account to check her balance. Yep, it was enough for tonight.

The dress she chose was new and a bit more daring than any she had worn before. After dinner she and Evie would go to Spider Joe's so it seemed fitting, she should wear it. The dress had been bought before she lost the weight from the last two semesters, but to Alice it looked good.

An Uber came for her and she met up with Evie at Spiro's Greek Restaurant for her birthday dinner. Her dad had loved Greek food and they had often come to the one in Green Valley because it was better than the one in Oakland. Roast lamb, rice pilaf, spanakopita, and stuffed vine leaves was one of her favorite meals. A small glass of retsina wine highlighted the flavors. When they finished another Uber took them to Spider Joe's.

The night had turned a bit chilly but both girls had colorful shawls to ward off the chill between the restaurant and the club. Once inside and seated in the VIP area the chill was gone and both left the shawls with their purses on the sofa where they had their drinks. Alice splurged and ordered a bottle of champagne. She thanked Evie for her gift, one of those delivered to the cottage that morning, and told her about the bouquets which she had received.

The flowers she failed to mention was the one from David Khoury. Alice still had not settled him in her mind. He seemed to be in her thoughts more and more since this morning. His face had been in the shower with her, was watching her while she combed and dried her hair, and while she dressed, he was there mentally wagging his finger in disagreement as to her choice of dresses.

Evie was enjoying the music but could tell her friend was in a mental quandary about something. She didn't think it was her school but then she had told her only the draft paper had been accepted. Certainly, she wasn't worried about the defense, she knew the material better than even some of the people on the thesis committee did. No, something or maybe someone was the problem.

Evie leaned toward Alice, "did you get more than the flowers from Paul? No dinner invitation or gift?" Perhaps he was her problem, but Alice simply nodded her head, no, that wasn't it. Well, he was the only one who she had been out with, oh there had been that doctor, the one who's dad owned those restaurants, but he had been at the aunt's funeral. Surely, he didn't mean anything to her.

Hmm, although, he had held Alice's hand a bit longer than necessary when he offered his condolences at the reception. No, it couldn't be him. Oh, he was handsome, but aloof and a bit too bossy for her tastes. She remembered when he approached them another time, they were in Spider Joe's and how he had tried to interject himself in the evening. But it was worth a try. "What have you heard from that doctor; you know the one who came to your aunt's funeral? "Evie said.

BINGO! The look on Alice's face said a lot. "Uh, he's uh, well he brought me some flowers but that's it." Alice stammered on, "he's not my type, uh, oh come on, let's just drop this and have some fun!" She grabbed a glass of champagne and downed it then poured another. "You need to catch up Evie, I only get to be twenty-five once in my life!"

Evie began to worry about her friend. She never drank to excess, but she could tell something was off. "Hey don't drink all of it, save some for me!" She filled her glass and hoped the spell over her friend had been broken. Two bottles of champagne later, she wasn't so sure.

Usually on nights like this, at Spider Joe's, she and Alice would have maybe two drinks, but rarely three. They would also do a lot of dancing, but tonight Alice barely moved from the spot she had inhabited all evening. A couple of guys had asked her to dance but it was if she hadn't heard them. Evie was getting worried about her friend.

Alice's phone sat on the table next to her glass. Evie picked it up and scrolled through the most recent calls. Noting there. Then, she looked at the contacts. Dr. David, hmm, that must be him. She laid the phone back on the table. "Come on, let's go. I've had too much to drink and we need to get you home."

Alice nodded, picked up her phone and texted the Uber to come and get them. She paid her bill and the two girls made their way to the entrance. A dark sedan pulled to the curb and David Khoury, dressed in medial scrubs and white doctor's coat got out. He looked at Evie and then to Alice. "Oh heavens! Why would you text me to come get you?" When Alice struck out at him he understood her condition when she passed out in his arms.

Evie looked at him, "good catch doctor. I think she thought you were the Uber. We were just going home."

David put Alice in the front seat and opened the door for Evie to get in the back. "Where do you live, I'll take you home and then take care of Alice." It wasn't so much a request for information as it was a command.

Several minutes later David pulled up to the front of the cottage where Alice lived. He felt it was better if he just left her sleeping. He retrieved the key to the door from her bag and lifted her in his arms. She put her arms around his neck and instinctively laid her head on his shoulder. "Alice, oh little Alice, what will I do with you" he whispered in her ear. "I've wanted you like this for so long, but not drunk. No, never impaired."

He took her into her bedroom and found a sleeping shirt on the end of the bed. He removed her shoes and slipped the dress over her head. "Hmm, Alice you are a beautiful girl, what do I have to do to make you understand you should belong to me?" Trying to redress her in the sleeping shirt was too much trouble so he put her to bed in nothing but the panties she had worn under the dress. She had been braless.

He sat beside her on the bed and watched her sleep. Her hair spilled over her pillow in silken waves. He leaned over and kissed her forehead.

In the living room he stretched out on the sofa. It was even more comfortable than some of the beds and sofas he would sleep on in the hospital. He had trained himself to sleep when he could be woken at the smallest sound from a patient and so he did in Alice's cottage.

Near six in the morning, he heard her stirring. He looked in the room and she had turned over and gone back to sleep. After a trip to the bathroom, David went to the kitchen to find out what the possibilities were for some coffee. He found the pot setup to make the coffee and pushed the on button to start its cycle.

A yelp from the bedroom brought his attention back to Alice. She was sitting up in the bed dressed in no more clothes than what he had put her to bed. He leaned against the door frame, "as lovely a sight as you are, you might want to put something on." He motioned to his chest.

Alice looked down at herself and grabbed the shirt, put it over herself and yelled, or at least started to yell but that was cut short when her head started pounding. The best she could do was a weak cry. "Go away!"

David went back to the kitchen and got Alice a tall glass of water and a couple of Tylenol. Striding back into the bedroom he handed the water to Alice and put the pills in her hand. "Take this" he commanded. She looked at the pills suspiciously. "It's Tylenol, for the headache and you need to drink lots of water to flush out the stuff you over-indulged in last night." He stood beside her until she took the pills and drank the glass of water. "That's better, another two or three glasses of water should put you right."

Alice moaned, "just leave me alone!"

"Ah, little Alice, that is not possible. I will stay her until I know you are out of danger from alcohol-poisoning. Why did you get yourself into that situation. Your friend Evie said you drank the majority of three bottles of champagne last night. Celebrating is one thing, but this cannot happen again. If you were mine, I would make damn sure it wouldn't."

Alice retorted, "well I'm not yours and never will be." She rubbed her temples. "Just leave me be!"

David sat beside her and pushed her hands away. He took his hands and began to massage her head. His hands slipped through her hair with ease and before long her head was resting on his chest, her eyes closed. "Little Alice why do you insist on pushing me away?" he whispered. "Can't you feel this connection we have? You belong with me and only me." Lightly he brushed her hair with a kiss.

She pushed herself into a sitting position again. "Look, I need to uh, uh, well, ..." He moved and let her get out of the bed to go to the bathroom. While she took her time, David went back to the kitchen and got another glass of water for Alice and another cup of coffee for himself. He met her coming out of the bathroom and she ran to her bed and covered her bottom half.

She took the water from him and he set his coffee on the night-stand when he sat on the bed next to her. "Did, uh, did you put me to bed?" When David nodded, she blushed and lowered her eyes.

David put his finger under her chin and raised her face up so she was looking in his eyes. "I'm a doctor, I see a lot of naked people all of the time. Very few who are as pretty as you or have the kind of breasts a man could get lost in, but it's all very normal for me to see people without their clothes." He noticed that when he mentioned her breasts she squirmed. Oh my, how responsive this girl was.

"Alice, are you still a virgin?" She pulled away from him and turned a furious red. Oh no, she was, he could tell by the reaction.

Shaking, Alice stammered, "you have no right to ask me that, that question! Go away, get out of here, leave me alone!" She was pushing him off of the bed and he landed on the floor next to her.

He grabbed her hands and pulled her down on top of him. In a quick deft move, he was on top of her and had her pinned to the floor. "Do you really want me to leave you alone, little Alice?" He covered his mouth with his. She parted her lips and he kissed her long and deep. She quit struggling instantly.

David stood and picked her off the floor. He put her on the bed and holding her two hands above her head, he straddled her. He again began to kiss her and with his free hand he caressed her body. She didn't fight him and as his hand brushed across her bust, he could feel her nipples harden under the shirt. Where the shirt ended and her little panties began, he stopped to see if there was any resistance. Ever so lightly he skimmed over the dip in her hip and to the top of her thigh. He looked down at her.

"Open your eyes Alice, I want you to look at me." Slowly she brought him into focus. "Now, that wasn't so bad, was it." Alice nodded. "Please little one, when I ask you a question, I want an answer. Tell me if you objected to me kissing you."

A quiet "no" escaped her lips.

"So, I think that is enough for today. You still need some rest and I have to call my service. I'll be in the living room." He put the covers over her and took his coffee cup. He kissed her forehead and closed the bedroom door on his way out.

Alice drifted off to sleep. She had never felt like this before and the kissing coupled with the massage had put her in a very relaxed state. Her last thoughts were of David. David the powerful, David the amorous kisser, David, just David.

In the living room, David checked with his hospital service and there was nothing that needed his attention. His mother had left a message on his phone to call her before church, but a look at his watch told him they would already be leaving church. He sat in the recliner and pushed it back. His phone was on vibrate and if he got any calls, it would wake him up.

Two hours later his phone started vibrating. The ID said Judy and he let the call go to voice-mail. He didn't want to talk to her right now. Quietly he looked into Alice's room. She hadn't stirred. Good, she needed the sleep, but she also needed something to eat.

George Khoury, his cousin, lived near his apartment. He called him and asked him to bring him a set of clothes and some food. He gave him the address and told him not to knock or use the doorbell. He didn't want Alice disturbed. David said he could see when his cousin would arrive.

Thirty minutes later George delivered everything David had asked for and left. David got a quick shower and changed. He found an unopened toothbrush in the linen closet and brushed his teeth; shaving would come later.

Alice came out of the bathroom just as David was putting the food on the table. "Do you feel up to eating yet?" David asked her. "You are much too skinny and you need to eat to help get your body back to normal."

She stood in her sleeping shirt and panties. "Why doctor, is there something wrong with how I look?" She said in a teasing tone. "I thought you liked my body just the way it is." Before she could react, he had her pinned to the wall again.

This time he had stretched her arms above her head and held her two hands in one of his. "Don't play with me Alice, I know how to play right back." He covered her mouth in a kiss that left her breathless. "This is not a game for me and until you know the rules, you should be careful about teasing me." He let her arms drop. He still had one hand. "Now come over here and we'll eat."

This time she didn't argue but let him sit her down at the table. He put food on her plate and also on his. "Now, girl, eat."

GRADUATION DAY

Evie and Alice stood in line with the other Master's Graduates. They both wore the same kind of robes except for the hoods that were color-coded to the different disciplines. Evie's parents were sitting in the audience and beside them, David and Paul. The two men who were vying for Alice had called a truce while they helped Alice celebrate her achievement. Evie's father still caste a wary eye at each of them.

The relationship between Alice and David was much more cordial but she was still wary of him. He made her feel things that she had never dreamed of feeling before but he didn't treat her like any of the guys she had ever dated. He never tried to do anything more than kiss her and only then when they were alone. Paul, however, kissed when he picked her up to take her to dinner, at dinner, and again when he brought her home. But he just didn't kiss like David, did nor stir the kind of feelings David did. Perhaps David was correct when he told her Paul was not the one for her, but was David right?

Anyway, now was not the time to think about such things. The line was moving and she could see Evie walk across the stage and receive congratulations from her department head. One more group and then it was Alice's turn to walk with her fellow historians.

She hoped the graduation gift she had gotten for Evie would make her friend happy. It had been their habit to always take a mini vacation somewhere between the semesters. Since they hadn't gone anywhere during the two thesis semesters and this would be Alice's last semester in school and Evie was headed to Florence for two years, Alice wanted to make it a trip to remember.

At last, her name was called and Professor Fisher handed her a rolled-up diploma. "Excellent work Miss Blake! I enjoyed working with you." She switched her tassel from one side to the other, she had graduated with honors and for her, school was done!

The graduation party was at Evie's. Her parents had insisted and Alice couldn't really find a reason to turn them down. She had the gift for Evie in her purse and after the dinner which her mother had had catered, a cake was produced with both of the girl's names on it. Alice handed Evie the envelope.

Evie looked at Alice in a questioning way, "What's this?"

"Well, open it and find out." Alice said. As Evie tore the envelop open, she explained, "I thought since you had to start your course in two weeks, we could go over a week early and stop in Paris for a couple of days. Then I can go with you and stay in Florence with you another couple of days before you have to get down to another bunch of studying."

"My god, these are first-class!" Evie looked at Alice. "I'm, I'm speechless!"

"Hey, if you got to go, go in style girl!" Alice told her.

Paul moved to Alice's side, "if you had told me about this, I could have helped you, at least of the Florence part of the trip. I wish I could get a week or so off of my job to go with you and show you around."

Alice turned to Paul, "Uh, that's fine, can I talk to you after the party?"

Paul's eyes lit up, "hey, how about now?" He took her by the elbow and led her outside to the patio. After closing the door, he turned to look at Alice. "So, what do you want to talk about." He reached out his hand to rest it on her shoulder.

Alice stepped out of his reach. "Paul, I have enjoyed our coffees and dinners, I really have, and you make a wonderful friend, and if I had a brother, I would want him to be just like you. I want to be you friend, but I just don't think we could be anything more."

Paul flashed a look toward the house. "So, it's David then, the great doctor." His voice dripped with sarcasm and Alice wasn't going to take it.

"Look Paul, it isn't anybody. I'm just not interested in anything more than being friends right now. I've just finished a period of intense study and lost the last of my known family in the process. I don't know what is next for me, but I have to find that out and romantic chaos is not part of what I want to deal with." He bowed his head. "I'm sorry to say this to you but you had to know."

With a great deal of strength, he stood erect once more and smiled at Alice. "I hope you find what you are looking for, good night, and again, congrats on the graduation." He didn't even walk through the house to leave but exited by the gate at the side of the house.

For a few minutes Alice stood alone. She had much to do and she was hoping the trip to Europe with Evie would help her sort out exactly what and who was most important in her life going forward. First-class or coach, the flight time was the same and there should be time on the going and returning parts of the trip to give her time to search her mind for some of the answers she would need going toward the future. Finally, she turned to rejoin the party.

Evie was the first to notice Paul was not with her. "Where is Paul, did you leave him outside?"

Alice nodded, "No, he is gone."

Evie gave her a look, "What, he's just left or he's gone gone?"

Alice grimaced, "gone, gone." She didn't see the happy smile that momentarily flashed on David face, but Evie did. "Anyway, I think maybe I'm ready to go. I've had a busy few weeks and I need to decompress." Looking around to Evie's parents she thanked them again and got her purse from the hall table near the front door.

David came up behind her, "I'll take you home." It wasn't a question or request, he was going to do it, period. Dutifully Alice stood by the car door and waited for David to open it for her. Not a word was said on the way to the cottage.

David pulled to the curb in front of the house. He turned to Alice, "You should have told me you planned on leaving with Evie next week."

Alice looked at David. "There was no reason to tell you. I can now come and go as I please. Right now, I am going to bed. Thank you for the ride home and for attending the graduation." She opened the car door and had her key in the cottage door before David could get out of the car. She didn't even look back.

EUROPE

Preparations were coordinated between Evie and Alice for their big trip to Paris and Florence. Each girl was allowed two large overseas suitcases and Evie had a lot of things she wanted to take to Florence for her school. Alice put some of the things in her luggage because once Evie got to Florence that space would be freed up so she had room to put anything she might buy.

Three days before the pair were due to leave Alice got a call from the banker, Mr. Jefferies. Someone was wanting to buy the fifteen acres she and Evie had seen a few months prior to Alice's birthday. "The buyer wants a quick sale and it's all cash. It can close in a matter of days. The price is more than fair and you won't have the burden of paying any more taxes on it in the future."

Alice told the banker to go ahead with the sale but that she would be in Europe for the next week. "Can we do DocuSign on this?"

Jefferies assured her it was the preferred way the buyer wanted to handle the transaction. "I'll tell the real estate agent he can proceed then. Have a wonderful trip! The proceeds will go in your current account and you can decide what you want to do with it when you get back."

Evie's parents took both girls to the airport to see them off. Evie wouldn't be coming back home for the two years she was supposed to be in Florence but her parents were planning a trip to see her near

Christmas. As for Alice, it was nice to have someone to say goodbye to her.

However, as she turned to get in the security line David came striding up to Alice, put his arms around her and before she could object, kissed her long and hard. "Did you think I would let you go without saying goodbye little Alice?" he whispered in her ear. "Remember who you belong to and don't let anyone else take liberties with you while you are gone. I will know if they do because you can't hide anything from me. Now, smile and let me kiss you again."

Alice was transfixed. David had this power over her and he could tell it made her squirm. She raised her mouth to him so he could kiss her again and this time she melted into him. Evie's mother and father turned away out of a sense of giving the girl some privacy and Evie was busy looking at her shoes. She had never seen anything like it before and especially with Alice. Hmm, they would make a very handsome couple. They would need to discuss this on the flight. It would beat watching a movie!

David released Alice and steadied her. "Have fun and don't forget to tell me everything that happens. I'll try to call you every day." A peck on the forehead and he went back to his car. Only then did Alice really start breathing again.

The dinner service had been cleared away and both girls sat with a white wine. Evie turned to Alice, "Okay girl, spill the beans on David. What have you two got going? I thought he was going to make love to you right there in the airport!"

Alice sipped her wine. "Evie, I don't know. When he kisses me, he just takes my breath away, I get wet, uh, you know, down there, and I don't know what I'm doing. Ever since he got us from Spider Joe's a few weeks ago he's been like this. He put me to bed, spent the night in the living room on Aunt Dorie's recliner, and then made me some breakfast."

Evie looked surprised, "Did he ..."

Alice blushed, "get your head out of the gutter, no he didn't! But he did ask me if I was a virgin. I, uh, I was mad but embarrassed and I guess he figured out the answer to that one. He just keeps saying I belong to him and that he is the man for me. I hope this trip away will give me some space to think."

Evie seemed to be satisfied with Alice's answers. It was Alice who needed to do the work on figuring out what she would do next. She knew she didn't want to stay in the cottage so it should go up for sale when she got back. There were some repairs that needed doing and she had to get rid of a bunch of stuff but that shouldn't take more than a couple of months.

Where would she live? The property her father had bought was sold and as the banker put it, for a very good price. Her personal needs didn't extend beyond a couple of bedrooms, ample bathrooms, and a garage for the Shelby. The money she got from the land would cover a modest condo in Oakland and some of the money her Aunt Dorie had left her would get the cottage in excellent repair to get the best price.

But, did she want to live in Oakland? She could live anywhere. She wasn't tied to a job or school. She wasn't married and had no plans or prospects for doing so in the near or even mid-term. So, what to do?

Alice had finished her wine and pushed the tray table up after the flight attendant had taken the wine goblet. She closed her eyes and in no time, she was being kissed and caressed by David in a dream. However, what had started as a mildly erotic dream soon turned into a nightmare when David had her bound, blindfolded, and tied to a tree, a long whip was hanging from his belt. He was pacing around her and growling in her ear that he would show her to whom she belonged.

Her eyes flew open but the images stayed with her. She even felt like she recognized the tree she'd been tied to. She signaled for another glass of wine and stared out of the window. The night was cloudless and a half-moon was riding low on the horizon. Stars filled the blackness but there were no answers for Alice there.

Alice eventually gave sleep another chance and this time it was dreamless and more restful. Evie woke her when the breakfast service began and the pilot announced they were two hours from Paris.

The temperature and fact it was a lovely day in the French capital gave the planeload of passengers a great forecast for the start of their respective trips.

Evie and Alice had both studied French since high school and the first few years of undergraduate study. Speaking with the officials in the airport and the taxi driver was not difficult. The car ride to the hotel led past some major landmarks and the girls enjoyed the trip.

The hotel staff was efficient and the small suite Alice had booked was ready for them. The bellman left their luggage and after Alice had tipped him, he closed the door so they could appreciate the beginning of their stay. One of the reasons this particular hotel had been chosen was for the small balcony each room had and the views. The basket of fruit and bottle of champagne which came with the suite gave the girls something to sip and nibble on while they took in the scenery.

It was a two-bedroom suite that was connected by a sitting room with desk, wet-bar, and comfortable sofa and chairs. The desk had chargers for their phones and laptops which both girls carried. The bedrooms were also equipped with phone chargers on the night-stands. Everything was in soft colors and was tastefully decorated.

They were discussing the sleep now option versus staying up and going to bed at the local time and trying that to avoid the inevitable jet-lag they both knew would hit them in the next day or so. "I think taking a nap now, getting up about lunchtime, and then doing some sightseeing this afternoon would be the best." Alice opined. "Maybe we could even be up later this evening and experience Paris at night."

Evie was shaking her head, "no, one of the students who I will be studying with in Florence sent me some tips to making the transition easier between U. S. time and Italian time, he said not to sleep until night and it will be easier to get on a regular schedule earlier. He's from Chicago and that is what he had found to be the best way to reorient his body-clock."

The ringing of the room phone interrupted the discussion. Alice was in the chair closest to the phone and signaled to Evie, she would answer it. "Hello, hello," a click on the line and the call was connected. Again, she said, "Hello!"

"Good morning, little Alice. Did you have a nice flight?" It was David.

Alice was surprised, "it must be the middle of the night there, what are you calling me for?"

"Ah, now, did you think I wouldn't be concerned about you? I'm just leaving the hospital after a rather difficult surgery and was hoping to catch you before you and Evie left the room to go sightseeing." It was his voice; it could be so soothing and even hypnotic.

Alice tried to shake off the spell but just his voice could make her wet. God, what was he doing to her. She hoped her voice sounded steady, but she wasn't sure. "We, uh, we are discussing right now weather to take a nap now and stay up later tonight or just power through today and sleep at a regular time. We are trying to avoid jet-lag."

She could almost hear David smiling, "well, my little Alice, speaking from a medical point of view, try to stay awake as long as you can tonight and then go to bed. I would like you to text me about how that is working for you, it will help me in the future." In the background Alice could hear the hospital PA system and David abruptly had to say goodbye, "They are calling for me, I have to go. Take care of yourself, text me often, remember, you belong to me."

Alice looked at the telephone receiver. Put it down and rejoined Evie on the balcony. "Who was that" Evie said. "You sure were intense on that phone!"

"Hmm, it was David. He said we should try to stay up as long as we can tonight and then go to bed, uh, medically speaking. So, I guess that debate is over. "Looking at the champagne bottle, "I hate to leave this, but any more of that and it won't be a question of sleep or not, sleep would win."

They both grabbed their phones from the chargers and sat at the desk to plan what they would do next. A map of the area around the hotel was helpful and they took it with them in case they got lost. A concierge stood behind an elevated desk near the front door. Alice had an idea.

Pulling out the room key, she showed it to the man and said, "my friend and I are staying in this room for the next couple of days. Is there any chance you could get us tickets to the Follies Bergères?"

The older man chuckled, "at this short notice, it would not be possible. Tickets for their shows are sold out months in advance. If there is another Follies, maybe one of the lesser-known ones would suit just as well." Alice was shaking her head, "is there anything else you want to see? I can suggest something if you give me an idea of what you want."

Alice thought for a moment. "The Museum at Les Invalides? I understand they have some of the artifacts from the reign of Napoleon?" She saw the big smile on the man's face, "maybe arrange the taxi and give us some suggestions for lunch while we are there."

The concierge, M. Balat, was able to make arrangements for the taxi and gave them a small map with some interesting eating establishments nearby which he had circled for them. "I think you will like any of these cafes. I hope you both enjoy yourself."

The girls did have fun. The part of the Invalides they toured was interesting and they both learned something they had never known from school. The had a great lunch and afterwards they let a taxi take them to some of the fashion house shops. Alice found a scarf which she wanted to give Evie's mom and a handbag she could use when she went out. Evie didn't like any of the items so they left and returned to the hotel.

M. Balat was still at his place near the door and greeted the girls when they returned. "Which of the cafes did you like? Did you have a good time at the Invalides?"

Alice set her packages on the floor near the desk. "We had a great time. I wish more of the history of Europe, France, and some of the historical figures were taught without political bias in the United States. There are things we learned about Napoleon that go beyond the label of him being nothing more than a despot."

M. Balat smiled, "eh, it took generations in this country before anyone would come out and give simple praise for Napoleon the man. He was always hailed for the Code' Napoleon, our legal code, and the redesign of Paris, but as long as the friends of the Bourbon's were in any power, Napoleon the man was denigrated." He shook his head, "but, I might have something you girls might like."

Evie lit up, "what do you have?"

"A Canadian couple had tickets for tomorrow night, but they have to return to Montreal tomorrow morning. Before I turn them back in, how would you like to spend a romantic evening on the Seine with music, food, and the beautiful sights of Paris after dark? I have two tickets for the Bateau Mouche!"

Alice looked at Evie, they had both seen films with the famous boat in it and people having dinner. Evie nodded. "We'll take them!" Alice reached for her bag and pulled out her credit card.

M. Balat smiled, "I don't take payment, we put it on your room bill and you pay when you leave if that is acceptable to you?"

She smiled, "that is fine, thank you! It would be better if we had someone to go with us, but I'm sure we will have a great time. But now we need a place to have some dinner. Any suggestions?"

M. Balat produced another map. He looked at it for a few seconds, "tell me, what you want to eat. Do you like or have you ever had escargots? French style of course."

Evie and Alice had both had them in New Orleans and they were good. A nod from Alice and Evie said, "I think the French style of escargot wins!" M. Balat circled the restaurant.

It looked to be a bit far on the map and M. Balat quickly told them, "Yes, you could walk there, but it would be better to take a taxi. If you tell me when you want to leave, I will have a car here for you. Also, it wouldn't hurt if I called the restaurant and asked if they need a reservation for you."

Alice thought about it, "seven thirty alright with you Evie?" Her friend smiled, "M. Balat, I think we'll do the seven thirty if that works out."

The concierge made a note of the time and told Alice that if anything changed, he would call the room. The girls thanked him and took their packages and tired feet to the room.

Both girls showered, changed, and sent texts to their family or friends. Evie had promised to keep her parents informed about her whereabouts and Alice sent a simple text to David, Evie and I are eating snails tonight. She didn't expect a reply but within seconds her phone notified her of a new text.

Enjoy the escargot. I love that restaurant and wish I was taking you there myself. I think more texts throughout the day from you would make me feel better about this trip of yours. David was beginning to be a bit too controlling for Alice's tastes but she appreciated that he seemed to be genuinely concerned for her wellbeing.

Tomorrow night Evie and I have reservations for dinner on the Bateau Mouche. Alice replied.

Who are you going with? Evie and anyone else? Remember you belong to me and I won't share you with anyone else! David was just short of shouting in all caps.

Calm down! It is just Evie and I. I don't belong to you! I don't know where you got that idea from but maybe this trip will finally break your mental bond with that delusion and understand I belong to no one. Good night!!! Alice put her phone on vibrate and stuffed it in her bag. As the girls left the suite to take the elevator down to the lobby to get their taxi, the room phone began to ring.

The taxi was waiting as M. Balat had promised and the girls left the hotel for dinner.

The food was fantastic and the girls stayed out longer than they had anticipated. The manager of the restaurant called a taxi for the two and they arrived at their hotel close to midnight. The front desk clerk had several messages for Alice, all from David, who had been trying to reach her by phone. She had ignored the vibrating of her phone throughout dinner. "Please inform the switchboard that we are going to sleep and don't want to be disturbed by any phone calls," was all Alice had to say on the matter.

In the room, Evie and Alice put their phones on the chargers next to their beds. Alice noticed several attempted calls and some texts from David and Evie told her she also had a couple of texts from him looking for Alice. "Can you please tell your boyfriend not to go through me looking for you?" Evie said, "He's really getting obsessive about you."

Alice sent one text to David before she got into bed. David, don't bother Evie when you are looking for me. We are both going to bed and don't keep pestering me. Remember, I don't belong to you, I belong to myself!

Within seconds a reply arrived, don't make me come over there and get you! You do belong to me and please don't forget that! My hand just itches to turn you over my knee!

Alice read through the text twice before answering, Again, I don't belong to you and why would you want to turn me over your knee?

David replied, because little Alice, naughty girls that don't listen get a spanking!

Pervert! was Alice's one word reply. She turned her phone off while it was charging and snuggled down in the bed to sleep. She had forgotten how tired she was. The last time she had really slept had been in her aunt's cottage in Green Valley. The tiredness helped erase the problem of David from her mind and within minutes she was fast asleep.

The first full day in Paris was a real treat. The weather was great and the sounds of the city as it came alive was much different than they had imagined. Coffee and tea were brought to the room along with a selection of fruit and bread rolls. Butter and a jam neither Evie nor Alice could identify made for a quick breakfast. Showered, changed, and with phones and maps in hand, the two wanted to go to the Louver.

The front-desk had a single message from David but it simply said he hoped they had fun and enjoyed the day. When Alice had turned her phone on before breakfast there had been a similar text message but she didn't answer it. In the taxi going to the museum, she sent a simple message, we're fine, slept well, going to Louver. Alice smiled when no reply came back.

Evie and Alice spent most of the morning surrounded by some of the best art man had ever produced. The 'winged victory' at the top of a staircase, the small, greenish-hued Mona Lisa, and the armless Venus di Milo, with countless treasures mixed in made for an exhausting first half of the day.

M. Balat had told them about a café at the #5 Rue Daunou called Harry's New York Bar. It is a famous Paris landmark from the age of Jazz music and as M. Balat stated, "Yankee baseball hotdogs." An outside table at the café gave the girls room to stretch out and rest from the morning. In the afternoon, they were only two blocks from some of the other Paris fashion houses and they tried shopping again.

Alice had never been big on shopping. She knew what size she was and had no problem ordering staples online. Evie, however, was the daughter of a world-class shopper. The days of doing simple Christmas shopping was enough to last a lifetime for Alice, but Evie felt it was part of who her mother had trained her to be and she took full advantage of the training.

Alice didn't find anything of interest except a wildly overpriced dress which she didn't really think fit her all that well. Evie was the one who hit the jackpot. Hermes's was having a scarf sale and she found two to take to her mother for an upcoming birthday. Alice would take them back to the States with her and give them to Evie's mom on her big day.

Both girls wanted plenty of time to get showers and change before the ride down the Seine that evening so they hailed a taxi and returned to the hotel. There were no messages from David and a look at her phone also assured her that there were no texts there either. Alice smiled to herself, so maybe David had taken the generous hints she had been giving him!

Before Alice and Evie left for their dinner on the Seine, Alice asked M. Balat to make reservations for a taxi in the morning to take them to the airport for their trip to Florence. He assured them the car would be waiting for them after they had their breakfast. He also called them one to take them to the boat for their dinner.

Paris at night via the river was magical. The music was the perfect background to the food and the scenery. Alice had read somewhere that the food was not Michelin Star quality but it was more than adequate for the girls. They drank wine and watched as the people walked along the banks of the Seine and some of the monuments, like the Eiffel Tower were lighted for the night. All too soon however, they were back at their hotel, and getting ready to sleep.

Early the next day, with their suitcases packed, and phone and laptops recharged, they sat on the balcony eating their last meal in Paris. The bellboy took the cases down and Alice went to the front desk to sign the bill. A commotion behind her made her turn around. David was striding towards her.

Before she could move or even register what she was seeing, he had her in his arms and was kissing her. She tried to struggle but the kiss depended and she surrendered to him. Evie was behind her and cleared her throat to get David's attention.

"Ahem, we have a plane to catch! Nice to see you to David. Fancy seeing you in Paris!" Evie said. David finally let Alice come up for air, but he held her by the wrist and kept her close to him.

"My bags are already in the taxi; I've told the bellman to put yours in also. We have plenty of time to make the flight, we'll be in Florence in no time!" He smiled down at Alice and whispered in her ear, "I told you I would come over her and get you but evidently you didn't take me seriously. Big mistake. I still think you need a spanking."

Alice was still recovering from the kiss and shock of David's arrival. He held her wrist as he walked her and Evie out of the hotel. M. Balat had seen the kiss and smiled after them. "Ah, to be young and in love like that!"

Traffic to the airport was not as bad as Alice had thought it might be. The early morning planes headed back to the U.S. with the planeloads of tourists always started much earlier in the day and the mid-morning flights were more inter-Europe or EU in nature. The plane ride from Paris to Florence was not bad and Alice, Evie, and David all sat on the same row in First-class.

The hotel had been chosen because it also had a wonderful balcony with each suite where they could sit out and enjoy looking over the tops of the houses and churches in the older part of the city. It was supposed to be close to the lodgings where Evie would be staying for the next two years while she worked on her Ph.D. in Latin. David had the suite next to theirs.

The two suites shared a balcony which was divided by a short wall. David was undeterred and was sitting on the girl's balcony with an open bottle of wine before Alice and Evie were even out of their shoes. Evie decided she wanted a shower first and left Alice and David alone. Evie pulled Alice aside before she went into the bathroom, "you need to talk to him and get this figured out. Either you are in with him or you're not but you can't be on the fence."

When she heard the water running in the shower Alice went out to the balcony. "David, why did you follow us here? I've never given you any indication that I am even interested in you. What is your point?"

David handed a wine goblet to Alice, "little Alice, you tell me every time I kiss you how much you want me. I can read your body and when I talk to you your body gives me the same message. I know your mouth may say no but your body is screaming yes." He patted the seat beside him on the couch. "Come here and sit with me and I'll show you."

Alice sat on the front edge of the seat. David put his arm around her waist and pulled her to him. "Hmm, that's better. My women don't tell me no, in fact that word is banned in my house."

Her eyes flashed at him, "I am not one of your 'women' so I will tell you no when I want to. You have got to get over this idea that you ow …" Before she could finish the word, his mouth was covering hers in another deep kiss.

David could feel her squirming beneath him and could tell when it turned from defiance to wanting. He held her in the kiss for a long time and used his free hand to pull her onto his lap. She sat facing him when he finally released her from the kiss. She rested her head on his chest before righting herself and standing up. "That is not fair! We need to get this over with so Evie and I can enjoy our vacation before she starts her courses next week."

David pulled her down next to him, "Alright, sit here and we can discuss this. Look, I worry about you and want to keep you safe. I had a few days of vacation and wanted to be here with you. If it is good with you and Evie I will just tag along and enjoy the sites with you. Is that going to be a problem?" For once he looked all innocent, but the twinkle in his eye said otherwise.

Alice didn't catch the twinkle. "Can you please keep your hands and mouth off of me?"

David looked in Alice's eyes. "If you can honestly tell me, you feel nothing for me, then yes, I will, but it has to be honest and I first get to kiss you again before you answer." Without waiting for her to speak he had her in another deep kiss. This time there was no struggle, just a squirming that told him she had to be very wet for him.

"So, little Alice, be honest. Did you or didn't you feel that?"

Alice lowered her eyes; she couldn't look at him. He had a way of boring into her with those eyes of his like he could see everything she was thinking. He took one of his long index fingers and raised her head so he could indeed fix her in his gaze. He could see it, it was there, and if she was honest, she would admit there was something between them.

"I don't know what it is, but yes, there may be something." He took his finger away and was about to kiss her again when she pulled back and stood up in front of him. "But you have to get over this idea that I belong to you. I belong to no-one, including you, and if I can help it, I never will." She went back in the room as Evie was getting out of the shower. "Leave now, I'm going to take my shower."

Half an hour later, showered and dressed. Alice found David gone and Evie on the balcony. A knock on the door and David was standing with a very distinguished man, about David's age and build, and he introduced the man as Dr. Amara Dal Bianco. "Amara was in medical school with me. He lives close and I thought you and Evie might like to have dinner with us this evening."

Amara's English was excellent but Evie also spoke with him in Italian which was impressive to him. When he saw Evie, his eyes lit up and he had a genuine smile on his face. "I hope you are not attached to anyone because I might just have to steal you!" He kissed her hand and tucked it under his hand. "Please have dinner with us, it has been a long time since I've seen David, but you are a beauty for me. Please say you'll come."

Amara with Evie securely in his grasp led the way to a small restaurant near the hotel. "I think you both will like this place. It is very Florentine and the people who own it are a good family." Seeing Amara, the owner led the four diners to a quiet table and a couple of servers brought bread, oil, and wine. David asked his friend what the specialty of the house was and it was ordered for all of them.

Conversation flowed freely around the table and once or twice Amara reached up and took a tendril of Evie's hair which had slipped out from behind her ear and put it back where it belonged. It was an intimate gesture and Evie didn't even notice it but Alice did. Amara go up to talk to someone in the kitchen and Alice leaned into David and whispered in his ear. "He's your friend, please tell me he's not married with a bunch of kids at home."

David laughed. "Not to worry. Amara has never been and isn't married. Do you think I would bring someone unsuitable here to meet Evie. You said she would be here for two years. He might make a good friend for her and help to keep her safe. Her father and mother would probably like to know there was someone here looking out for her." David whispered in her ear, "The only relationship you need to think about is the one between you and I, little Alice."

When Amara returned to the table the servers took the dishes and replaced them with coffee and brandy. Tiramisu was brought out for each of them and the staff retreated. Amara put a small bite of the dessert on a spoon and gave it to Evie to taste. "Mm, wonderful, it tastes noting like the one you get in America." He then gave her a sip of brandy.

"You see how the flavors meld together? The combination of the two gives a depth to the dessert most people never experience." Amara's brandy, coffee, and all but a small corner of his dessert was untouched. He looked at his watch. "I hate to say good-night, but I have an early surgery in the morning. I have to leave you now but Evie, will you let me take you to dinner tomorrow night?"

Evie nodded. "I would love that."

Amara looked at David, "Oh, you can both come too, but I especially want to take Evie to dinner. Do you think eight is good?"

David laughed, "eight is just fine my friend. Good luck on your surgery tomorrow."

David walked Evie and Alice back to their room. At the door, he took Alice's hand and Evie went inside and let them have their privacy. "Let me come to your room tonight. I want to have a chance to talk to you without other people around."

Alice knew she shouldn't but she told him if he wanted to come for just a few minutes, well, he could.

David brushed a kiss on her lips and waited for her to enter the room before going to his room in the suite next to hers. David put on a pair of pajama pants and placed a couple of things in his pockets of the robe he also wore. When he came over the low wall on the balcony the door to Alice's room was open but Evie's was closed and no light shown from underneath the door.

He caught Alice about to get into bed. He put the blindfold on her and laid her down on the bed. He had a scarf which he used to tie her hands together above her head and fastened them to the headboard, all before she knew what was happening.

"I hope you don't need this tee-shirt anymore." Both hands ripped it up the middle and he laid her breasts bare. She was wearing a pair of panties which didn't last but a few seconds. He put his mouth over hers and the resistance again turned to cooperation. "You see little Alice, you want me." Taking his index finger, he checked her sex to see how wet she was. He put the finger in his mouth to taste her. "You taste so good! You are wet and you want me, don't you." Alice nodded. "That's not how this works. I don't respond to nods, you tell me yes or no and beware, I don't like the word no."

Meekly and barely a whisper, "yes."

"See, that wasn't hard now was it." She could feel his hands on her, intimately and probing. "You are still a virgin and I am not going to take that from you until you beg me to do so. But that doesn't mean I'm not going to teach you about your body and what I can do to it."

He slid down her and began kissing her pubic mound, his tongue found her clit, and he parted her labia with his fingers. He was careful with her, he didn't want to disturb her virginity, that was a prize he would take when she was ready to accept him as her Dominate. Now though, he brought her to orgasm with the expert use of his tongue and she writhed in pleasure.

David untied her from the bed, freed her hands, and removed the blindfold. "You see, everything is still intact. Now kiss me and I will say goodnight." Alice put her arms around his neck and pulled him to her. For the first time, Alice kissed David and it felt good, for both of them.

When Alice got up to put on another tee-shirt and panties David told her not to. "I want to know you are sleeping naked in the room next to me. I will dream about how I caressed your body and made you cum with my mouth. No, Alice, don't cover that perfect body." He reached down to pull the covers over her but left her breasts bare. "I want to suck at those breasts like I did at my mother's. They are too beautiful to keep from me." Then he was gone and Alice fell asleep with his smell all around her.

David's Story

Well before dawn David was back in Alice's room. He sat in the chair near her bed and watched her sleep. Never had he taken a sexually inexperienced girl as a submissive. He'd also never had to train one from scratch. The ones he'd had before had all been in the lifestyle for long enough that they had been trained by another Dominate/Master. He knew she was a natural to this, he'd seen it when she was taking care of her Aunt Dorie and from what her aunt had told him, the years of care she had given her mother before she died.

Alice Blake was worth the work it would take to make him a superb sub maybe even his consensual slave. He wanted her and he would and could wait for her to come to him, kneeling before him, and giving herself to him. That was his dream and what he was working to achieve.

Alice stirred but then settled into a deeper sleep. David sat forward in the chair, elbows on his knees, thinking about his life. It hadn't always been easy but he was in a good place now and the new house he was building would be the perfect place for his life with Alice.

Sitting back in the seat, he looked back at how he had become what he was. Growing up he was always into one mischief or another. Both of his parents were busy with the first restaurant and as the number of eating places went from one to two to four, he saw less and less of his father. His mother was never a strong woman, but she had done what she could to help her husband get his various businesses off the ground.

Alex Khoury had a large network of relatives upon whom he could call on to work for him. Cousins, a couple of aunts and uncles, all were offered the chance to leave the war-torn and ravaged country of their birth, Lebanon, to make a new life in the United States. It was all done legally and with the help of a good immigration lawyer, most of the management of the restaurants were family members. There was also an incentive for some of the younger cousins to get an education because if they worked in one of the restaurants, there was help with tuition and flexible hours for them to work and study at the same time. Two lawyers, three accountants, and two nurses later, there was someone in the family to help out those who needed it.

David was the only son and while he had worked in the flagship restaurant for a brief period of time, it soon became apparent he was not cut out to be a server of any kind. He was in middle-school and about to go into high school when Uncle Maurice arrived. He wasn't really his uncle by blood, but his father's father had been best friends with his father. When the friend died, Maurice came to live with Alex and his brothers and sisters where he was treated like family.

Maurice was a fighter. Starting during the long years of the Lebanese civil war when governments didn't exert power all over the country but militias ruled their little fiefdoms along religious or ethnic lines, Maurice had been part of the fight. He was no more than a child when he first picked up a Kalashnikov and guarded one of the check-points of the militia area with an older fighter. He didn't get much schooling from books but he learned what it took to live off the street, survive an attack by a rival group, and take an oath to his militia that he would defend unto his death.

By the time Uncle Maurice had immigrated to America, Alex Khoury had but one job for him, tame David before he destroyed his future. One of the smaller restaurants had an apartment above it and it was into this two-bedroom accommodation Uncle Maurice was installed with just enough furniture to sleep on, a table with two chairs to eat at, and an old sofa to relax upon. Maurice didn't want nor need more than that.

The first day after school had let out for the summer, David and a small satchel of clothes was deposited outside of Maurice's apartment door. Alex sat in the car and explained to the young David that enough was enough, Uncle Maurice was his last chance. "Make the most of what he will teach you."

Inside the nearly bare kitchen, Maurice had put two quarters on the table. "David, hm, we need some bread for our lunch. Take those two quarters and bring some from the store across the street."

The boy plopped down on the chair across from the old man. "Can't you get it?"

Quicker than the boy could think, Maurice was out of his chair and had the boy's face on the table and one of his arms behind his back. "If I want any back talk from you, I'll ask for it. Now, bread, market, go!" He released David and the boy scooped up the coins and was gone. Maurice watched from the window as he went across the street and into the shop. Less than a minute later he was on his way back to the apartment.

Maurice was at the door as the boy came up the stairs. "See, that wasn't so hard. You need to learn to follow orders, well, among other things, but it's a start." The training of David Khoury had begun.

David remembered how he hated Uncle Maurice, well, until he started to really find out what his uncle was trying to teach him. That summer turned into an adventure. Maurice was strict but fair. He never made David do anything that would bring disrepute on himself or the family. One of the first things he was taught was about the importance of family and making sure everyone was safe and out of harm's way. Respect for his parents, loyalty to them, and learning to live in such a way as to honor them. And, although Uncle Maurice was not a religious man, David went to the nearby Greek Orthodox Church. By the time it was the day before classes at the local high school were to start, David Khoury was ready to return to his family.

If this was all that Uncle Maurice had taught him, well it would have been enough and more than his parents had expected. However, it was on a visit to his uncle's apartment one day in his junior year of high school which would send his life in a much different direction. He knocked just after three in the afternoon but didn't get an answer. He was about to leave when he could hear shuffling from behind the door. He turned and knocked again.

Slowly the door opened and a long curtain of blond hair and half of a pretty face looked at him. He couldn't see the body, but a timid voice asked him what he wanted. "I'm David and I'm looking for my Uncle Maurice."

"Oh, David, he talks about you. Please wait, he will be right back," with that the door closed. David heard someone coming up the stairs and recognized the tread as that of his uncle.

Turning, David said, "Hi, uncle, uh I don't know who she is but she said to wait for you here."

Maurice grunted, "Mina, her name is Mina and she shouldn't be opening the door." He reached into his pocket and pulled out some coins. Handing them to David he said, "Go across the street and get some bread."

"Yes uncle." David went across the street and within minutes was back at the apartment. Maurice was at the door. He invited David to sit on the sofa and tell him why he had come. "We got out early today and I wanted to come and ask you if I could stay here this coming weekend. My parents are going out of town and I don't like to be in that big house by myself."

"Aren't there any staff in your father's house?" Maurice asked. "Yes, you can come, but things are a bit different here." He looked toward the kitchen, "Mina, come in here."

A barely audible "yes, Sir" could be heard from the girl. Eyes lowered, she looked at neither Maurice nor David. Dressed in a simple shift dress, she stood straight and had her arms crossed over her waist.

"Sit" was all Maurice said. The girl pulled a cushion from behind the couch and sat cross-legged near Maurice's side. He stroked her hair and she put her hands, palms up, in her lap as she sat quietly. Looking at David Maurice said, "Mina lives here with me. She is my sub or subordinate. I'm her Dominant. I have had her for about six months now and we are both doing fine." Maurice gave Mina's hair a slight tug, "Tea, girl, and be quick!"

Gracefully, Mina rose from her cushion on the floor, put it back behind the sofa, and went to the kitchen for the tea. Minutes later she reappeared with a tea tray which she placed on the table next to Maurice's chair. She gave the first cup to her Dom and then asked David how he took his. Once she had finished serving the tea, she again took the cushion to sit on.

While Maurice explained to David the concept of the Dom/sub dynamic, he stroked Mina's hair and at one point even brushed across her generous tits. David wondered how he could get a sub to do all of his work! But when he asked his uncle, the idle fondling stopped and Maurice looked angry.

"It takes years of work before you can even think of owning a sub. You don't even know who you are, how can you even hope to get someone else to buy into your vision when you don't know what it is? No, boy, you'd best forget about what you've seen here." Maurice escorted David to the door. "You're not ready for this world, much less my world."

David turned to say something. "Look, I can give you some books to read, but just keep this between us. If you have questions, I will answer them, but don't you dare think you can take on anyone until you figure out who you are." Maurice closed the door as David retreated down the steps.

That weekend, when David stayed with his uncle, Mina was not there. He didn't want to ask his uncle, but when they sat down to eat that night, he told him Mina was visiting her family for the weekend. He also gave David a list of books he could find in the library that described the world of BDSM and the D/s dynamic within that world.

Maurice warned the boy to keep what he was learning to himself. "I will answer any questions you have, but please remember that what you are reading is that particular author's view of D/s or M/s." He then asked about David's schooling. "I hope you are keeping your grades up. Your parents are determined you are going to university. I don't want to find you are slacking in your work while you try to learn this."

David assured him the lessons were being done. "I can do more than one thing uncle. Please let me learn from you."

Thus started David education in the world of mastery and dominance. Maurice should not have been worried about the study for university. What David was learning from Maurice was the kind of self-searching and discipline he would need. As David got older and his uncle took him to some of the kink-clubs he had never known existed near his home base, he learned about how to use whips, canes, floggers, paddles, and other toys for impact play.

Throughout his undergraduate years he studied on two tracks, pre-med and Master/Dom. His uncle gave him tasks to perform which helped him hone in on who and what he was. He discovered he had a sadistic streak, but it was not overly cruel or violent, he grew to love the pain/pleasure aspect of BDSM.

The summer before David would start his last year of undergraduate work, Maurice invited him to stay for a few weeks at his house. Maurice had long since moved from the initial apartment and had found an old house he was fixing up while he lived there. David never did know what Maurice did for money, when he asked his father, the older Khoury simply shrugged his shoulders. Wherever the funds came from, Maurice now owned a much larger house and the money to do the repairs.

A room in the house was being made over into a private dungeon and Maurice was getting a friend he knew to make much of the furniture for it. The walls were painted a dark green and pin lights in the ceiling could be adjusted to focus on specific items. David helped his uncle with the work but when they were not doing that, Maurice had David working on his vision and personal expectations of what he wanted and how he wanted to live.

Writing these things out was not an easy process and a red pen in his uncle's hand was savage to his lists. "Focus boy, in a year you will be in another city, away from me, studying medicine and I want you to know about yourself as much as possible. I won't be there to guide you and you must promise me you will not try to take on a girl before I say you are ready."

David made the promise. He knew he wanted the kind of life his uncle had shown him and if it took waiting until his uncle deemed him ready, then he would. He had seen what the relationship could be between a Dom and his sub and he craved that for himself.

Maurice had moved to the big house because he had a new sub whom he was going to marry and officially collar. David had seen at least three women in the past, but when Lala came to live with his uncle, he could tell the chemistry between the two was much different than any of the girls he he'd had before.

Lala was a beautiful lady of about thirty years-old. She was medium height and slight build but with generous breasts and curvy hips. When David was visiting, she wore a simple shift dress which buttoned down the front and nothing else. She never sat on the sofa or chair in the living room and waited for his uncle to give her the nod to sit at the dining room table. She called his uncle 'Sir' and never looked directly into his or anyone's eyes unless directed to do so.

She lived in the house full-time and even with construction being done in several of the rooms, kept the house immaculate. Lala was an excellent cook and would often make a dinner for his uncle and some other couples who were also in the lifestyle of D/s or M/s. When David was invited for these dinner parties, he sat and listened to the other Doms or Masters talk about various aspects of their lives. Their subs and slaves would help Lala serve or cleanup then eat their dinner in the kitchen before the night's entertainment would begin.

David marveled at how these men sessioned with their girls. Maurice was the perfect host and Lala an exquisite hostess. It was these men who would stand with Maurice when he officially accepted Lala as his submissive. Their wedding would be the day before and David was anxious to see both ceremonies.

The Khoury family, well, at least the older generation who remembered who Maurice was, came to watch him get married and stayed to celebrate the happy event. The men marveled at the young woman he was marrying and the women wondered why he hadn't chosen someone closer to his own age. The happy couple left to honeymoon at Maurice's house in preparation for the collaring ceremony the next day.

David always marveled that Lala was so totally different in public than she was in private. However, the closer he watched, he began to pick up very subtle signals between the two. She always stood facing his uncle, waited for him to signal her to sit, or any number of small nods or winks which he used to control her behavior.

The day after the wedding the newlyweds were up early. Lala put a wonderful breakfast on the table and then cleared and cleaned everything before the other Masters and Doms arrived to help prepare for the acceptance and collaring ceremony that night. The subs and slaves of the men came and helped Lala prepare for her part in the ritual.

The men busied themselves moving some of the furniture in the dungeon so a space in the center of the room was cleared. A couple small tables were placed to hold various items which would be used and one of the men went out to buy some dry ice for the cold branding which would mark Lala as Maurice's sub.

A couple of the girls made platters of sandwiches to feed the men. The dinner for the ceremony would be before it had taken place and it was being catered. Once the noonday meal was cleared and cleaned up the girls turned their attention to Lala and preparing her for the evening.

At seven a catering truck arrived with food which was put in the kitchen to be heated or removed from the fridge when it was time to eat. With the feast done, the men gathered in the dungeon dressed in their finest dress leathers or formal wear. Maurice was not a leather-man so he was dressed in a tuxedo.

Promptly at eight all but two of the subs/slaves entered the room and sat or kneeled on cushions at the feet of their respective Dom/Master. Each one of the girls wore the same color and style of robe. They were black with slits up the sides and were open in the front. Made from a transparent fabric, nothing could be hidden from either their Doms/Masters or the others in the room. The lights in the room were dimmed except for the one over the center of the room.

A light shown at the doorway and two attendants brought Lala into the room, stood her in the middle under the spotlight, and retreated to kneel on cushions before their respective Masters. It was time for the ceremony to begin. The first part was the reading of the contract which would bind Lala to Maurice as his sub. It wasn't a binding legal document, but in the eyes of all those in that room, it was an oath and vow more solid than anything either would sign. All of the parts were read aloud and after each paragraph or section Maurice would ask his kneeling girl if she agreed to the terms.

The various parts and terms of the contract had been worked out between them over many months of preparation for this single night. It detailed Maurice's responsibilities to Lala and vice versa. When the final paragraph was read, Maurice told Lala to rise. One of the Doms moved a small table to stand beside the couple. On it was a basin and a knife. The Dom pricked first Maurice and then Lala's finger and let the blood run into the bowl. His sub came with bandages to bind the wounds. Red ink was poured into the bowl and mixed with the blood.

Maurice looked down at his girl, "Lala, if you agree to this contract, sign it with our mixed blood." Lala stepped forward and in the silence of the room, the scratch of the quill pen she used to sign herself over to her Dom could be heard by all. Next, Maurice took the same pen and signed on the line above his sub. The Dom who had put the table beside them removed it and took his place back in the circle.

The two attendants who had brought Lala in the room then stood beside her and removed her robe. Lala stood before the entire group in nothing but her downcast eyes. Maurice took his index finger and raised her chin. "Kneel before me and accept my collar."

Gracefully, Lala knelt before her Dominate. One of the Doms in the circle approached with a pillow carrying a velvet pouch. Maurice removed his collar from the bag and took the tiny Allan wrench that came with it. He opened the collar, placed it on Lala, and using the wrench, locked it in place. The only time it would be removed would be for medical purposes or if she was released from her Dom. Maurice pocketed the wrench and would add it to his key ring later.

Maurice took his newly collared sub's hand and raised her up. The ceremony was not yet complete. Leather cuffs were locked on Lala's ankles and wrists. She would wear some form of cuffs 24/7 and Maurice had gotten her some new ones to wear around the house and others which would be suitable for wear in public. Two of the men who stood in the circle came forward and led Lala under a chain that hung from the ceiling. It was lowered to accommodate her.

Lala's hands were raised above her head and one of the men, a very experienced rigger, used ropes to secure each of Layla's ankles to fasteners in the floor. Her legs were opened as far as Maurice had directed. Everyone in the room could look upon he pubic area. Nothing was hidden. Another Dom brought a small table with the bowl containing the dry ice and a slush of water and alcohol. Maurice donned a pair of heavy gloves and took a pair of tongs to immerse the brand he had designed. The laser cut metal block stayed in the solution for the requisite amount of time and then Maurice removed it and placed it on the right inner thigh of his new wife and sub.

For fourteen seconds the cold brand marked her as his. She screamed in pain and tears ran down her face. Once the brand was removed, the rigger removed the ropes on her left leg and one of the subs, a nurse, bandaged the area where the brand had been placed. In a few weeks it would heal and would stay for a good five years when it would again be renewed in a recommitment ceremony. The rigger removed the ropes on the right leg. Lala stood; head held high, proud she had endured this for her Dom.

Maurice came to her, released her hands from the chain, and took a ring from his pocket. He placed it upon Lala's right hand. It was a simple gold band and was inscribed with that day's date. The date of his collaring, and signing the contract which bound them together. He wrapped her in a blanket, picked her up, and carried her to a couch where he put her in his lap and gave her the after-care such an intense ceremony needed.

David had found the whole day moving and compared to the marriage ceremony, he could tell by looking at Maurice and Lala, it was more to them than anything so far. If there was ever any doubt in his mind about the lifestyle, it was vanished on that day. He would follow his uncle's teaching and guidance because he wanted to have the same kind of relationship Maurice had with Lala.

The weekend before the final year of undergraduate study began, Maurice invited David on a picnic. Lala packed a basket of food and Maurice took his bag with selected 'toys' to entertain himself and Lala. David had no idea where they were going but a sign they passed read 'Clearwater' and it wasn't long after that Maurice turned down a lane that disappeared in a bunch of trees and undergrowth. David was sure his uncle was lost but he kept driving until the lane opened into a lovely field of wildflowers and ended at a lake.

Maurice and David unpacked the things from the car and Lala set out the meal. There was cold roast chicken, potato salad, slaw, and deviled eggs. She had also made some of Maurice's favorite Lebanese dishes and the meal was filling and just the thing for a fine late summer day.

Maurice took his toy bag and walked to one of the trees. He motioned Lala to join him and he instructed her to take off her dress. Lala never wore anything but dresses and always sat in a particular way as Maurice had instructed her. She had nothing on underneath her clothes. Maurice took the heavy leather cuffs out of the bag and put them on Lala's ankles and wrists. He then took a rope and had Lala hug the tree while he joined the cuffs together with the rope. He then took two shorter pieces of rope and spread her legs apart and secured them together around the tree trunk.

He took his flogger, a buggy whip, and a paddle from his bag. Going back to the car, he got his six-foot whip and put it beside the other toys. Next, he put a blindfold on Lala and whispered something in her ear. She squirmed.

Maurice stepped back to where David was watching. In a low voice he said, "Did you notice how she reacted when I whispered in her ear?"

David looked at his uncle, "Yes, what did you tell her?"

"I told her I was going to use her. Why do you think she reacted the way she did? Come on boy, you need to learn to read women or you'll never make it in this life."

"Well, she was aroused?"

"If I were to check her right now, she would be wet. And not just that, the anticipation of what I will do is going to make her wetter. One of the things you need to know is what reactions words, movements, a look, or even a caress can bring. You have to learn to read women and love them if you want to make this a effective way to live."

Maurice waited another few minutes, each minute adding to the buildup of Lala's imagination of what her Dom was about to do to her. He started off with the flogger and then moved to the paddle. He had turned her white ass a bright red and before he put the paddle down, he rubbed her red welts and then added his open handprint. He again whispered in her ear and she groaned and squirmed against her bondage.

Taking a single finger, he checked her and found she was very wet. This time he growled in her ear, "don't you dare cum unless I tell you that you can." He took the buggy whip and laid a line of strips down her back. She was groaning and he decided it was time for the big whip. He took it, unfurled it, and cracked the air a couple of times with it. The effect on Lala was a tensing of her body. Maurice caressed her body with his free hand until she relaxed.

Maurice stood back from Lala and gave her a lash across her thighs. The second landed just above the first on her buttocks and the third just above the second. He gave her six more lashes and then coiled his whip. Lala was quietly sobbing. He whispered in her ear again, took the flogger and covered the lashes. He caressed her between strikes and after every few would again whisper to her until she again squirmed. He went up to her, and stood covering her body. He held her and ordered her to cum. She exploded as he held her. When the waves of orgasm had passed, he undid the ropes that bound her feet and hands, he wrapped her in a blanket, and sat holding her in his arms.

Almost an hour later she donned her dress, Maurice removed the cuffs and put them back in his toy bag along with the rest of his things. With everything packed in the car, they drove back to Maurice's home. He told David he would try to see him in the next week or so but he and his girl were going to have a nap. David had never seen a session which had been as moving.

Graduation from his pre-med courses was shortly followed by the start of medical school in another state. The time he would have off between semesters and any free time would be severely limited during med school and then his residency in cardiology. David did not leave his study of Master/Dom nor lose contact with his uncle.

David kept up a constant correspondence with Uncle Maurice throughout his training. He was directed, by his uncle, to a small group of Doms/Masters in the college town where he was taking his medical degree and then again in the city where he was working on his training to be a cardiologist. He never let his grades waver or his 'other' life interfere with his grueling work schedule.

Before he finished the specialty and was to take his boards exams, he received word from Lala that his Uncle Maurice was ill. David got permission to travel home to see his uncle. Getting a letter from Lala was a first and David was afraid in what condition his uncle may be. He went straight from the airport to the house Maurice had fit to his special needs.

Lala opened the door and greeted David with the same grace and calm she had always shown to guests to her Dom's home. She took David's coat and suitcase then led him into the big bedroom on the second floor. There, propped up on pillows, was Uncle Maurice.

"Uncle," David said, "why didn't you tell me you were sick." Looking at him, David could see he was about fifty pounds lighter, a sallow color, and his once lush hair hung in lank strands from his fast-balding pate. David sat on the edge of the bed and took his uncle's hand.

Maurice turned to look at the boy, "I am so proud of you. The rowdy little trouble maker your parents sent to me is now about to become a respected doctor. I could not be happier for you if you were my own child." David could tell it was taking a lot of his uncle's strength to speak, but he insisted on proceeding. "I also believe you will be ready to find and take a sub or slave of your own. I've had good reports about you from the men you meet with each month."

David gave his uncle a sip of water from the cup he had beside the bed. "I do want you to finish your studies, establish your practice, and then begin your search. It may take you a long time to find your special girl, but when you do, she will be your own special gem. My Lala is my heart and if I have any regrets, it is that I didn't give her permission to have a baby when she had wanted one. Now, I will leave her with only this house to remember our life together. She can live here, rent free, for as long as she wants and then it goes to you. Watch over her and take care of her. Keep her as safe as if she was your own blood auntie." Feebly, Maurice grabbed the front of David's shirt and he looked him straight in the eyes, "Swear to it!"

"I swear uncle." David said as he took Maurice's hand. "I will see to it she is safe and secure." David could barely keep his voice even. He knew he would cry later, but now was not the time. He sat holding his uncle's hand until he went to sleep.

David found Lala in the kitchen. "How long has he been like this? Why didn't he tell me he was sick?"

Lala put a teapot on the table and David sat down. She remained standing until David asked her to sit with him. She poured tea for them and said she would answer any questions she could.

"Master," she saw David react to that, "oh, yes, at our last renewal ceremony he finally took me as his consensual slave. Anyway, Master began having something like flu a couple of months ago. It was flu season and he would never get the vaccine, so he thought he would just take what he usually did for flu and ride it out. But it didn't go away, it just hung on and he continued to get weaker and weaker." Lala sipped her tea and continued, "I finally got him to go see a doctor, actually a kink-friendly doctor who was Master of jasmine. Well, he ran some tests and he took some scans at the hospital."

David was starting to worry about what she would say next. "It's his pancreas. It's inoperable and stage IV. If he lives" by now the tears were running down her face, dripping onto her shift, and she couldn't go on. She lowered her face and after a couple of minutes had composed herself. "Uh, if he lives for more than another month or so it will be a miracle. He doesn't want to go anywhere; he wants to die at home. He does have hospice coming every few days to check on him and I will be with him no matter what." Lala was again overcome and cried openly.

She blew her nose and righted herself in the chair. "He is more than a husband to me; he is my Master. I know you, of anyone in the family, can understand what a bond that is. When I wrote to you, he said he wanted you to stay here if you could. I don't know how long you have, but any time you can spend with him, with us, will be a blessing."

Lala got up from the table to remove the tea things. She looked at David, "I know he has told you that he thinks you are ready to take on a girl of your own. He has also told you that first you need to finish your studies and establish yourself. Master has asked me to also talk to you about what it is like from the perspective of a sub/slave. While you are here, if you will like, I shall be happy to do as he has asked."

David stayed with his uncle for another two days but then had to return to take his board exams to be certified as a Cardiologist. After the exams, instead of going with the rest of the residents to party or get some much-needed sleep, David got the first plane back to be with his uncle.

The short time he was away made a big difference in his uncle's situation. By the time David was again at his side, Maurice could barely speak. In a raspy voice he pointed to the dresser, "my, uh, my keys boy." David got up from the chair he was sitting in and got the keyring his uncle always carried. He handed it to his uncle.

Maurice held the keyring for a while and at one point David was almost sure he had slipped into sleep but he was just gaining strength enough to talk. "The collar, my collar, take it off," he pushed the keyring to David, "wrench, re, remind her it is mine. Dungeon, deface the brand, put in the case with the contract, and the collar, bury with me. Take collar off when I die."

The energy he had to talk was gone. Maurice slipped into a deep sleep, aided by the morphine the hospice nurse had hooked him up to and which gave him a steady amount to counteract the pain of the cancer. David quietly cried by his uncle's side until he too, exhausted from worry, exams, and the approaching end of his residency, finally took over and he slept.

Lala, knelt on a cushion beside her Master's bed. She held his hand and laid her head next to it. She also cried herself to sleep.

Later that same night, Lala awoke when she felt her Master's hand caressing her hair. Quietly he bid her, "come girl" and she laid down next to him. She was holding him as he breathed his last. David checked his pulse and confirmed he was gone. Lala sat on the bed holding Maurice's hand and raised her hair from her neck so

David could remove the collar which had never left her from the day Maurice had put it on her. David took the collar and left her crying beside his uncle.

In the dungeon he defaced the brand as his uncle had wanted and put everything in a small wooden box which would go into the coffin with his uncle. He phoned the hospice nurse and informed her of his uncle's passing. He also went to sit with his uncle's body.

The funeral was appropriately somber and attended by both family members and the Master and Dom couples that had been so close to Maurice. Lala was swathed in black and at one point he worried about her health. After the service and burial, David had a chance to sit with her in the house. "You can live in this home for as long as you want. I know he left you a monthly stipend and some other things but if you ever need money, help, or just someone to talk to, please let me know. I've been talking to the local hospital and they are interested in having me join the Cardiology Department, if I passed my boards. I will be here for you."

Lala looked at him with red-rimmed eyes. "Thank you and I will be staying, at least for the foreseeable future. I have a sister in Kansas, she was widowed last year and she has asked me to come stay with her. I may visit her, but as for staying, well …" She trailed off in thought.

David left her to her thoughts and went to the dungeon, locked the door with the key from his uncle's keyring, and left the house. Lala stayed in the house until after everything was settled on Maurice's estate. As his wife she was well taken care of and his will was very clear on the properties and funds he had left for David. A codicil on the will was in Maurice's own hand and was a personal letter to David.

Maurice had tried to buy the property he had found in Clearwater where he and Lala would go on picnics and play. He wanted David to find the owner and buy it if he could and if he ever wanted to build on the property, to make sure he didn't cut down Lala's favorite tree. It was more than ten years before he bought the land from an old estate. The tree would be safe.

David looked out of the window and calculated it was about an hour until dawn. Alice was sleeping comfortably and it was taking all of his willpower not to lay down beside her. The lessons of Maurice and the long talks with Lala played in his head. He would wait for her because trying to rush her might just make her run away from him.

Quietly he left her room and going back over the short wall on the balcony, returned to his room to get a couple hours of sleep. He was sure neither Alice nor Evie would be up before eight when breakfast was to be delivered to their suite. Slipping into bed he soon fell into a deep sleep.

FLORENCE

David was showered and changed when breakfast was delivered to the girl's suite. He tipped the waiter and set up the meal so it would be ready when the girls came out to the balcony to eat. He could hear the showers running in each of their bathrooms and it took no time for them to emerge and take the proffered coffee from David's hands.

Alice came out first and David worried she might be angry with him about the night before. He was pleasantly surprised when she smiled at him and thanked him for the coffee. "Did you sleep well little Alice?" David asked. "I hope you had wonderful dreams and a restful night."

"Hmm, I slept very well. I think I remember you giving me a, uh, sleeping pill before I slept." She blushed and lowered her gaze. "I enjoyed it immensely."

David put his arm around her waist and took the coffee cup from her hands. Setting it aside, he pulled her to him, and gave her a long, deep kiss. "I enjoyed it also," he whispered in her ear. Alice squirmed in his embrace but not to get away from him but to mold herself to his body. "If you are a good girl, we can see about a repeat tonight while Evie is having dinner with Amara." He kissed her again and then released her.

Evie came in but she had seen the second kiss when she was coming through the door to the balcony. "Good morning, David. Alice. So, what do we have on for today?"

The three talked about various things to do in Florence but reminded Evie of her date with Amara for dinner that evening and the fact she would be moving into her permanent lodgings for school the next day.

Just short of nine there was a knock at the door. David's friend Amara was holding a large bouquet of flowers which he gave to Evie and Alice took to put in a vase. "I finished my surgery and the patient is out of recovery. I have the whole day to take all of you, or if David has plans for Alice, it would be my great pleasure to escort Evie on an introductory tour around Florence."

David took charge. "I think we would all like a tour, well, at least until lunch time when I think Alice and I will have a nice, quiet meal together." Amara took Evie by the hand and David claimed Alice.

The tour was indeed something that only a native of the city, and one who loved his city, could take a group of friends on to introduce them to the magic of Florence. They first went to the Pitti Palace to see Michelangelo's David and the Pietà. He then took them to a market where fruits, vegetables, and all sorts of items could be bought. The spice market was especially enjoyed. Finally, he drove to a hill that overlooked the city. Before them, the ancient and still vibrant city of Florence was seemingly laid at their feet.

The two couples, David and Alice, and Amara and Evie stood and looked at the city stretched out below. David looked at his friend, "you know, all through residency you would talk about your home with such love. Now I understand what you were saying. It really is amazing. Thank you for sharing this with us."

"Oh, my friend, I have so much more to show you, but now I think you want to have lunch alone with your beautiful lady," he looked down at Evie on his arm, "and I am going to get to know this lovely lady better."

David took Alice's arm as he led her down a couple of side streets near the hotel. The hotel concierge had recommended a quiet little family restaurant which was well within walking distance. He memorized the map and around the next corner a brightly colored awning over a portion of the front of the building proclaimed this to be Suzie's Café. Small tables were placed outside, but David was more interested in eating inside where he could take his time with Alice.

A buxom lady in her early forties greeted Alice and David at the door and seated them at a booth near a window. The menus were in English and Italian and David ordered for both of them along with a white wine and a full-bodied red to go with the main course. Looking at Alice, "it is better to have our main meal at mid-day and we can eat lightly this evening." He chuckled, "that is if you still want to have dinner with me."

Alice blushed, "Yes I want dinner with you, as long as you select the perfect desert for me."

He took her hand and turned it palm up. "I think I can find just the right one. In fact, we may even try it out this afternoon if we have time." He caressed the palm of her hand then lifted it to his lips and gently kissed it. David could feel her squirm in her seat and if he could have seen her thighs, he knew she would have them pressed together tightly.

The long talks he had with Lala after his uncle passed away were an added layer of information on the mind of a sub/slave. He was sure he could see this same mindset in Alice, but Florence was not the place to do more than become familiar with her and let her become comfortable with him. He wouldn't broach the subject of how he lived until he could show her his home and could answer the millions of questions she would have. He wanted all of her and no matter how long it took, he would put in the time and work to make that happen.

They had a leisurely lunch and almost two hours after they sat down, he paid the bill and they left the restaurant. The walk back to the hotel was slow and David held Alice's hand the whole way. Instead of taking Alice back to her suite, he took her to his.

It was a single bedroom with a sitting room. The balcony was the same as Alice's, but instead of being outside, he chose to sit next to her on the sofa. He wanted to kiss her and hold her but he didn't want her to be shy.

"Alice, will you do something for me?" he said in between kisses. When she nodded, he asked her to take off her bra and panties. "I want to feel you and hold you. Can you do this for me?"

She stood up and slipped her panties down and kicked them to the side. Then reaching around under her blouse, she undid her bra and pulled it off. David pulled her into his lap. Her skirt rode up around her hips and he lifted it up and caressed her bare buttocks.

"Mm, you have such a nice round ass. You don't know how much I would love to spank you!" He felt her squirm but she also started to pull away. "Don't be afraid Alice, it's all about pain and pleasure. It's something I want to show you in the future, but not right now. It's not the time or place. Now it's all about your sensuality and the ways you can use your body to feel all kinds of pleasure."

She settled in his lap and he continued to kiss her. He used his hands to explore her body. Pushing her blouse up above her breasts he kissed one nipple and then the other. "I could get lost in your breasts! I want to suck your nipples and make you cum. Someday I want to spend my time making love to you, but until you come to me and ask me to take your virginity, I won't disturb it. But as you know from last night, you can still feel pleasure in other ways."

Alice felt safe and warm in David's embrace. All animosity she had felt towards him was in the past and she hoped the closeness they were having in Florence would not disappear when they got back to their respective homes. She laid her head on his shoulder while he played with her breasts.

Finally, he set her next to him and went into the bathroom. Looking down at his trousers, he could see the wet mark Alice's pussy had made in contact with his leg. David decided to change out of his street clothes and put a pair of pajama pants and a short robe on. When he got back to the sitting room, Alice was where he had left her with her blouse pushed up to expose her generous breasts and her skirt around her waist which exposed her pubic area. God she was beautiful! His cock agreed and it took great willpower to ignore the feeling building up inside of himself and rationally stay with his plan of the conquest of Alice. Uncle Maurice's lessons were paying off.

David pulled Alice back into his lap and she laid her head on his shoulder again. Having conquered his desire to fuck her, he simply caressed her body and whispered in her ear. "You are so beautiful Alice, I want you so bad, but you're safe with me until you want to give me your prize." In almost no time, Alice was sleeping and David laid his head on her head and also slept.

The last of the sun finally pierced the room with golden rays as it set in the west. David was the first to wake and ever so gently he picked up Alice and laid her on the sofa. He went to the bathroom and came back with a warm washcloth to give to Alice to help her wipe the sleep from her eyes. Tenderly he woke her and kissed her. She sat up and also went into the bathroom.

Coming back to the sitting room, she retrieved the panties and bra she had discarded earlier and put her shoes on in preparation to go back to her own suite. David gave her a final kiss and told her to go dress for dinner. "I'm taking you someplace special this evening," was the only thing he told her.

Alice showered and changed into a short little dress that left little to the imagination. She was sure David would love it. David came to her suite to take her to dinner and his first reaction to the dress was swift and cruel. "Alice, that dress is totally inappropriate for this evening! Have you no sense of what a proper young woman should wear? Go, change it immediately."

Tears streamed down Alice's face. In her bedroom she stripped off the offending garment and riffled through her things to find what David might consider 'proper' for her to wear. A tea-length silk charmeuse dress in a dark green highlighted the color of her hair and was the perfect complement to her complexion. It also hugged her figure but it was better than the last dress.

When David first saw her, he came to her side and kissed her deeply. "This is my little Alice! Did you really think I wanted the world to see you in nothing more than a slip? I want to show you off, yes, but not look as if I was pimping you to every man whom you would arouse in that thing. I think more of you than that!"

Alice understood and silently vowed to herself she would never do anything to displease David for as long as their relationship, uh she guessed it was a relationship, would last. She slipped from David's embrace and got her bag so they could leave, "you said we were going somewhere special but at lunch you talked about a light meal tonight. I don't understand," Alice quizzed.

David chuckled, "you'll soon see. Amara is out with Evie and I want to take you to a special showing at one of the museums. He had tickets through his father and since he would be spending time on something he deems much more important to him; he gave them to me so we could enjoy the private showing. They will have champagne and hors d'oeuvres. I think you will like it."

A taxi was waiting for them when they exited the hotel and David gave the driver the address. "Amara said that some of the most influential people of Florence will be attending the gala. Mostly they are doners who help raise funds for the museum to acquire new pieces. Amara has already donated so he thought we would like to go instead of him."

The cab stopped before a very graceful but imposing building with a broad stairway leading from the street to the front door. A red carpet had been laid for the arriving guest to walk on and at the top of the stairs, liveried men stood at the glass doors and opened them to all who had an invitation. David paid the cab and took Alice's arm.

She had seen this kind of setup in films but never in real life. David set a slow, steady pace as they ascended toward the doors and the men who were guarding them. Dr. Amara hadn't only given David his invitation, he had written on the reverse side who he had given it to and asked that David and his guest be welcomed in Amara's place.

Gaining entry was no problem and once through the doors, a bank of cameras snapped their pictures. A man approached them and shook David's hand. "Welcome! You must be Amara's doctor friend from America. I'm Danniello Dal Bianco, Amara's father. He has spoken about you since you were both in medical training." The man shifted his gaze to Alice, "and this is the lovely Alice whom he told us about also." After kissing Alice's hand, he asked them to follow him to their table.

"My wife is anxious to meet the two of you. We had the honor of meeting with Evie this afternoon and she said the two of you have been best friends for most you your life." The round table they were taken to had three empty chairs and David and Alice were first introduced to Amara's mother before they sat down.

The room was a main hall of the museum where priceless baroque tapestries hung from the walls and various large busts of long-dead glitterati of that time in Florence's history stood on display. Danniello gave them a short introduction to the room and said it was used for dinners like this and also for wedding receptions. "When the program finishes, then there will be employees of the museum who can guide you to wherever you would like to go and explain the pieces of art. But you can also explore on your own if you wish."

"My wife, Breda, and I won't stay past the program, we have some engagements tomorrow in Rome and we must be up early to make the trip. For us it will be early to bed tonight but please, David, we want you and Alice to enjoy the museum for as long as it is open tonight."

David thanked them for their kindness. "Thank you, we will stay for a while, but tomorrow we are helping Evie to move into her lodgings for school. She will be here for two years studying and I know Alice wants to see her well settled before we go back to the States the day after."

"Ah, then tonight you must enjoy the artwork!" Danniello exclaimed. "My wife and I are hoping to get to know Miss Evie very well while she is here. My son is quite taken with her and there is no denying she is a beautiful young lady."

Alice smiled and said, "I can tell you from my long friendship with her she is indeed more lovely on the inside, her character, than on the outside. I am going to miss her while she is here but I'm happy she has your son to talk to."

A man at the head table tapped on the microphone before him and the chatter in the room quieted. The program began. It was all in Italian and although Alice didn't speak the language, she knew French so could almost understand the gist of what the man was saying. Danniello whispered the more salient things the man was saying to David. The most important aspect of the evening was the silent auction and another money-making part which involved men bidding on a dinner with one of several lovely ladies in the room.

Alice and David didn't pay much attention to the proceeding until a gentleman rose and in Italian said something to the emcee. People shifted in their seats and were looking at the table where Alice was sitting. A spot light shown on her but Danniello rose from his seat and in rapid-fire Italian said something to the emcee and to the gentleman who was standing. David whispered to Danniello.

"I regret, my friend, that the young lady is spoken for and is therefore not part of this. She will also not be here since she and her man are leaving for their home the day after tomorrow. Any of the other local ladies will, I am sure, be very happy to have lunch or dinner with you." Danniello finished his speech and then leaned over to David. "I suggest you and Alice might wish to leave when my wife and I go. We can drop you at your hotel which I think would be safer for Alice."

David nodded, "I think, by the look on that guy's face, he doesn't like losing. We would be happy to leave with you. My one priority is to keep Alice safe."

Servers began to move among the tables with drinks and platters of finger foods which were put on the small plates in front of each person on the table. Alice had never seen this kind of service before but it made sense. Instead of trying to juggle a champagne flute as well as a plate with food, spills and dropped food were kept to a minimum.

When the emcee announced the final numbers of donations for the night, he bid everyone a good evening and people started to mingle among the tables or head off to see some of the displays in the other parts of the museum. Amara's parents shepherded David and Alice out of the room, into the foyer, and down the outside staircase to a car waiting at the bottom of the steps. The ladies sat on the back seat and the men in jump-seats which faced them.

Amara's mother took Alice's hand. "Thank you my dear for being so calm over the whole mess. Michael knows not to do things like that but he just doesn't have an off switch when it come to a pretty girl. I hope this doesn't ruin your stay with us."

Alice laughed, "no worries, I could only understand a part of what he was saying and I'm glad there was no problem sorting it out. I've had a lovely time in Florence and, "she looked at David, "this is a trip I will remember for many years to come."

Danniello winked at his wife and smiled. The car stopped before the hotel and the driver opened the door so David and Alice could get out and Danniello could sit next to his wife. They had hugged and kissed in the car and David wasted no time in getting Alice up to his room.

"I want you to go to your room and change into something more comfortable. Remember how I wanted you this afternoon?" Alice nodded, "yes, I want you the same when you come back here."

Ten minutes later Alice knocked on David's door. He had also changed in to pajama pants and a short robe. "I left a note for Evie that I was here in case she came back and didn't find me in my room."

David smiled, "good thinking. Come little Alice, I have some food ordered. I wasn't happy with what we were offered at the museum so we will have some meats, cheeses, and fruits we can nibble on. While we wait," he handed her a flute of champagne, "we can enjoy the wine."

A large lounger sat on the balcony, just like the one that her suite had and it was under a canopy in case of inclement weather. The sky over Florence was clear and the temperatures mild for early Summer. Stars shone brightly through the light of the city. A moon was just beginning a journey across the sky. It was perfect.

The top Alice wore had buttons down the front which David had open in the first few minutes. Her breasts were sensitive and as David played with them, he noticed how she squirmed. He pulled at her nipples, rolled them between his fingers, and alternately sucked on them. A knock on the door got him off the lounger but not before he covered Alice's tits. "I'll be right back."

The serving cart was rolled to the French doors and David made a small plate of cheese and ham slices and another of some of the fruit which had been cut into chunks. He refilled their wine glasses before again taking his seat with Alice. He took a sip of the champagne and then before swallowing it, kissed Alice and transferred it into her mouth for her to drink.

"I want to feed you and care for you. I've told you before, you belong to me. That seemed to anger you in the past, but from the very first time I met you, I've felt you are the only woman for me. Can you understand now why I've said that?" David took a piece of fruit, a pitted cherry, and put it in her mouth.

"Mm, I think I feel the connection, but I've never really had a boyfriend and am not sure of what I feel." She took another sip of wine and continued, "I don't even know what this," she gestured with her hands to encompass the room and David, "this is? Am I a simple diversion for you in a foreign country or what? How will this, whatever this is, continue in the States when we return? I'm confused."

David pulled her into his lap. "Alice, this is what I have been trying to tell you almost since I met you. This," and he also gestured, "this is about us. Us together, us with a connection and a bond that will reach from my soul to yours and make us one." He pulled back and looked at her full on, "I'm almost hurt you would think I was so shallow as to make this only about a transitory fling. Perhaps when you learn more about my life and how I live you will understand better."

The exchange seemed to satisfy her. They took turns feeding each other and then it was time for David to return Alice to her suite and her bedroom. He locked the door then took her clothes off and pulled the covers almost off her bed. He had her lay down and he removed his clothes before laying down next to her.

For the first time she could feel what a naked body pressed against her felt like. David had a fine, muscular and toned body, much like the statue of David which they had seen at the Pitti Palace that day. His hands caressed her and tentatively she tried caressing David's body.

He moved between her legs and slid down so he could use his tongue to bring her pleasure. It wasn't long before he had her writhing and close to climax. He pushed her over into a giant orgasm which pulsed through her body. Before the last wave finished, he rolled her over until she was on top of him, her full body over him. He held her in an embrace which pressed her breasts into his chest.

Moving her back to his side it was taking all of his willpower to keep from being aroused. He almost lost the battle when Alice began to caress his chest and started to stray even lower. It was when she whispered in his ear, "isn't there something I can do for you? I've never done it before, but I've heard girls talk about it. If you tell me how it's done, I would like to suck your, penis, uh, I mean, uh, cock."

David sat up and pulled a pillow over his erection to hide it from Alice. "My sweet one. I'm happy you would like to do that for me, but I don't think you are quite ready for that yet."

Alice knelt facing him, she pulled the pillow from his lap showing his fully erect penis. "I think maybe you cock has other ideas about that." She pulled her hair back and leaned over him and put her mouth on his member. First, she kissed it and licked it.

When David understood this was indeed going to happen, he pulled her to him. "If you are going to suck my cock, you are going to learn to do it the right way." He sat on the side of the bed and had her kneel in front of him on the floor. "This is one of the better positions for you to do this. I'll help guide you as much as I can." She put the head of his cock in her mouth, sheathed her teeth with her lips, and began to apply some suction as she slowly moved it in further and further. One hand was used to hold it and the other cupped his balls. She began a steady motion which had him wanting to speed up her pace and also cum. His hands buried themselves in her hair and before long he was fucking her mouth. She was taking more and more of his shaft into her mouth and before too long he began to deposit cum in her throat which she swallowed, something which surprised him.

"And you say you've never done this before?" he whispered to her. "I don't think I've ever had a better blowjob in my life!"

Alice was still licking him clean. When she finished her jaw was a bit sore but she was happy. The salty, warm cum he put in her was her prize and she was happy to have been able to claim it. "I've never done it before, but I didn't say I hadn't seen it done on YouTube."

David pulled her up into his lap, "you can do that for me any-time. In fact, it will be part of your daily routine in the future, would you like that?" She rested her head on his chest and nodded. "Mm, little Alice, you are amazing and each day I'm more and more convinced you are the one for me."

All too soon David laid her under her covers and kissed her goodnight. "We have a big day tomorrow. Sleep well my dear." He dressed and was gone. Sometime much later Evie came in and checked that Alice was in her room and went to bed.

David was in Alice's suite bright and early the next morning to eat breakfast with the girls and help them get Evie settled in her lodgings. Amara came to take them to the house where Evie would be living for the next two years. Pulling up in front, it looked like any house in a middle-class neighborhood.

Evie rang the bell and a woman of about sixty years-old answered. It was her home and she supplemented her income by renting rooms to students who were studying under Professor Dell 'Abbate. She welcomed the group and took them to Evie's room.

It was a large bedroom at the back of the house and overlooked a neat little garden. It had a desk, chair, bed, and dresser. In the middle of the floor were the four large boxes Evie and her mother had packed and shipped via UPS. She added her suitcases to the pile. A small bathroom was down the hall and would be used by the owner of the house and Evie. Three other bedrooms on the upper floors were for the men who would also be in residence and they had a separate bath for that floor.

Amara introduced himself to the owner, la vedova Giannis, or the widow Giannis. He gave his contact information and asked her to call him if there were any problems. The fact he was a doctor and seemed to care very much for the American girl was not lost on her, but she reminded him she didn't allow men in the women's rooms or women in the men's rooms after a certain hour.

Amara smiled at that and said she was being a good chaperone as well as a careful householder for having such rules. "I feel safe with her in your house and under your care."

For the next couple of hours, the four busied themselves with putting things away and in the end the boxes were empty, the bed was made, and the suitcases and boxes taken to the attic for use when Evie would leave Italy at the end of the two years to go back home.

One of the things Evie liked about her lodgings was the fact meals were included in her rent. They wouldn't start until the beginning of the term which was in two days. If Evie was not going to be in the house for a meal, she needed to let her landlady know so she could adjust the menu, but until meals started, it was up to her to find her own food. Lunch was coming up and Amara and David wanted to take the girls for a good meal.

A small restaurant outside of Florence was a little more than an hour away and Amara enjoyed taking them in his car. The scenery was beautiful and as promised, the little café had a wonderful view of a vineyard and beautiful trees. They sat outside and Amara ordered for them.

"This is what we consider country cooking." Amara said, "The bread is made fresh every day and the sauces are made with fresh herbs. All of the vegetables are from the garden and they even have a house wine made from grapes grown on their land. I hope you enjoy this; it is one of my favorite places."

The meal was simple fare but well-made and the wine was the perfect pairing for the food. The owner gave them excellent service and his wife left the kitchen long enough for the young people to thank her for the lovely lunch. Almost two hours later they began the trip back to Florence. Amara and David left Alice with Evie and told them they would return in about four hours to take them to dinner.

Alice was happy to get a chance to talk to Evie on her own. It had been a few days since David had joined them and private time alone had been sparse. Evie went first, "okay so what is going on with you and David? He seems to be everywhere with you and since when did you start sleeping naked?"

Alice blushed, "David has been showing me some wonderful things he can do with my body. I told you he only needs to whisper in my ear and it makes me wet, well sitting on his lap, dressed, but with no panties or bra is marvelous. He's also," Alice stopped when she saw the look on Evie's face. "What, he hasn't done anything, well, I'm still a virgin if that is what you're worried about. He has made me orgasm," Alice rolled her eyes back in her head, "what he can do with his tongue is amazing! He's done it twice and both times has told me he won't take my virginity until I ask him to do it."

It was time for Alice to turn the tables on Evie. "So, what about you and Amara? He seems very taken with you and his parents are almost as enthusiastic as he is. I met his parents the other night, uh last night, and they really like you."

Now it was Evie's turn to blush. "He has been a perfect gentleman with me. He's, just, uh great! I know what you mean now about getting wet over a guy. He simply touches my hand and I'm soaked." Talking about him was also triggering the same response. "I don't know how long I'll be able to take this before I'm begging him to seduce me!"

They both laughed but understood that something was happening to both of them. Feelings they had long ignored while they worked toward their educational goals were being brought to the surface and the men responsible for these feelings were being careful with them and both wanted desperately to know where it would all lead. Were they just the first ones there and so reaping the newness of the girls awakening or were they really the 'one' for each of their respective girls. Only time would tell.

Until the guys returned Evie and Alice talked. They both knew that early the next morning Alice, accompanied by David, would be leaving for the United States. This was probably their last chance to talk, in person, until Evie returned to her home or if Alice would make the trip back to Florence. "Make David bring you back here or at least come for a few days yourself. I know Amara would love to have you visit." Evie said, "I'll miss all of the stuff we used to do and holidays with my parents or our little mini-vacations to the beach." She teared up and they hugged each other tightly.

As promised, exactly four hours later the men called for their ladies. The restaurant was not far from the hotel where David and Alice were staying and Amara was using his father's driver for the evening. "I don't have any surgeries tomorrow so I can have some wine this evening. Since the fines for drinking and driving in Italy are very strict using Papa's car and driver makes sense."

The place they went to had a much larger dining room than they had been to in Florence before. Music could be heard coming from a room adjacent to the one where they sat and Amara said it was where they could dance and sit at small tables and listen to the music while they drank wine. First though, food was at the top of the list.

The restaurant was owned by a Venetian couple so the preparation of the food, the spices, and wines would be a little different than what they had eaten so far. The conversation around the table was lively and Amara was telling Alice a funny story about his time in the United States.

"… and David came in just as the Chief Resident was finishing his speech. So how to hide the fact he was late and not get caught? He bent over and acted like he had just been bending down to pick up his pen. The Chief Resident couldn't remember if David had been in the room before that or not so he got away with it." Amara looked at David, "I always thought she had a crush on you, the way you would get away with stuff, amazing!"

"Not like that attending physician you studied under who just "happened" to spill the coffee down you scrubs and made you change in front of her? She just wanted to see you half naked!" David responded. "Anyway, I doubt you will ever see her again. She got married and is practicing in a small hospital in Iowa."

With the dinner over the men took their respective dates into the next room. It was dark but the stage and dance floor was lighted so it was easy to see the dancers. David warned Amara they should only stay for a short time. "We have an early flight tomorrow and it wouldn't be a very good idea to be rushed or impaired in the morning."

A slow song was being played and Evie and Amara, David and Alice began to dance. Having Alice in his arms David could feel the connection between them and when he whispered in her ear, he felt her squirm. Amara was doing something similar to Evie but for both of them the feelings were so new and their relationship was still in its infancy. Where they were going with each other, they didn't know.

David had talked to Amara that afternoon about Evie and was told he was very interested in her. "I think she is feeling the same way." When he saw the look on David's face he said, "Don't worry, I would never do anything to hurt her and I suspect she has very little experience with men."

"Alice is the same and I think you are right about Evie. They have been the best of friends since they were in primary school. They really never dated in high school or college. When I met them, they were both working on their Master's degrees and were entirely focused on finishing in the shortest time possible." The same thing had intrigued David when he first had contact with Alice. However, it happened, he was glad she was!

Amara poured more tea into their cups. They were in his apartment near the hospital and siting on the balcony which overlooked the back garden of the building. "I took Evie to meet my parents. My mother thought she was a nice girl and father was almost ready to start talking about grandchildren!"

David laughed, "I met your parents at the museum event that evening and it was all your mother and father could talk about. I think meeting Alice has sealed the deal for them." David took another sip of the tea, "the fact Evie is so fluent in Italian is also a big plus for them. I just hope everything happens the way the two of you want. Don't feel you are being pressured into anything." He sat his cup down, "you know, when I introduced you to Evie, I really didn't expect you would be this crazy about her. I just thought it would be nice for her to know someone here while she was away from home, but I think you really have the bug for her."

Amara nodded, "I've never met anyone like her. She is the only thing I think about from the moment I awake until I sleep and then I dream about her." He blushed a bit, "I have to admit, the dreams are a bit more graphic than they should be but they are my dreams."

David chuckled, "sounds like you have it about as bad as I do, but I've known Alice for almost two years and it has only been on this trip that she has even let me close to her. Think what agony I've had to endure, but for her, it is worth it!" He looked at his watch and recommend they go and get the girls.

The evening did end early and the driver left Alice and David at their hotel. Amara took Evie to her lodgings then went on to his apartment. David recommended that Alice should pack and he would do the same.

When he left her at the door of her suite, he kissed her and whispered to her, "I'll come see you in about a half an hour. I hope you will be ready for me." Alice squirmed in his arms and pressed her thighs together tightly. David felt it and smiled, "I know you are wet for me, finish your packing and I'll see you shortly."

As she packed her bags, Alice reflected on the way David affected her. The way he was making her panties wet she would only have a single clean pair to wear the next day when they both flew home. She slipped the ones she was wearing off and put them and her bra in the laundry bag in her suitcase. She laid out the clothes she would be traveling in, a mid-calf flowy dress and flats, but left noting out to sleep in that night. She liked the way David had started her sleeping naked and, weather permitting, would continue the practice when she returned home.

Home, she sat on the edge of the bed and took a few minutes to think about what home meant to her. She would be going back to her aunt's cottage but only to finish preparing it to be sold. She didn't really have a home any more. Evie would be staying in Italy, her family was all gone, what or who did she really have that she could call 'home'?

She sighed. David. David came to her mind. But what was he really? He felt like home but she just didn't know that much about him and what was he really wanting from her? Alice stood up and finished her packing. Maybe on the plane back home they could talk or she would have time to think. She heard the door to the balcony open and knew David was coming.

Much later David put his clothes back on, covered the sleeping Alice, and kissed her on the forehead. They had pleasured each other and he was still surprised at the skill she had in bringing him to climax with her mouth. Most of the girls he had known before were not really into sucking cock and didn't put as much effort into making it enjoyable for both of them. Alice seemed to like swallowing his cum and licked him clean after she had finished. He looked forward to the day when he could open her and truly take possession of all of her body. He wanted her to clean his cock of the cum he would put into her that would also be mixed with her own pussy juices. Mm, it was something to strive for!

One of the many things Lala had told him about being his uncle's slave was how much it meant to her to give him pleasure. He hoped that in the future Alice could see things in about the same way. There was no doubt that it was very satisfying to give Alice pleasure but she hoped that she would come to see giving was just as important as receiving. Many people missed that and thought it should be all about them.

Alice was awake and dressed when David and breakfast arrived early the next morning. The first rays of sun were just peeking through the curtains on the balcony and the bellboy had gathered the luggage from both of their rooms to take downstairs. After a cup of coffee and a breakfast roll the two left their suites and went to pay their bills.

The taxi ride to the airport was short and the flight was on-time. Alice and David had a few minutes to check out the duty-free shops but nothing really tripped their fancy. Alice didn't like to buy things just to be buying them and David was about the same. They both did most of their shopping on the internet.

As the plane taxied down the runway David took Alice's hand, leaned over, and whispered in her ear, "I look forward to our continuing relationship and hope you feel the same." He saw her shift in her seat as she clamped her thighs tightly together.

Alice whispered back, "every time you whisper to me you make me wet and this is my last clean pair of panties!"

David smiled and breathed in her ear, "so take them off."

Alice stared at him in surprise. "In public? What if I get something on my dress?"

"Yes, in public, but only I will know and as for the back of your dress, pull it up and just sit on the seat with your bare ass." David retorted, "also, sit with your legs parted. I want to be able to put my hand up your skirt and feel how wet you are. I always want to have full access to you whenever we are together." He saw her move her thighs apart as he had asked but she didn't move to remove the panties or raise the back of her skirt.

David pushed the call button and an attendant came immediately. "Yes sir, can I get you something? Champagne maybe?"

"I think it is a bit early for champagne, but coffee would be nice. A blanket if you have one also." The man left and David turned to Alice. "If you are a bit shy still you can put the blanket on while you remove your panties and your bra," he whispered. "I want to know there is nothing between us."

The blanket arrived and Alice used it to cover herself while she took off the panties and removed the bra. She pulled the back of her dress up and gingerly sat on the hygienic cover David had removed from one of the pillows in the bin over their seats.

While she was covered, he put his hand between her legs and indeed found her quite wet. He tasted her and then kissed her. "I love the way you taste Alice Blake. I want your essence all of the time." David smiled at her and continued, "I hope you feel the same. We haven't had a chance to talk, but that will be our next step. Right now, I just want to be as close to you as possible."

A steward brought their coffee and another attendant put a tray with a plate, utensils, and breakfast condiments on it. In less than a minute another server came with a selection of rolls, breads, and breakfast items for them to choose from. Orders were taken for those who wished a more substantial breakfast. For the next half hour David and Alice concentrated on their food.

It did give Alice a few minutes to think. Everything was moving so fast but she had no idea of where she was going with David, or what he intended the outcome to even look like. He hadn't mentioned love, or even like, all he had really said is that he wanted her with him, and as for any clue about what a future might be, she had no idea. Perhaps with them being in separate accommodations it might give her some time to process everything.

David could see that Alice was engrossed in her own thoughts. He hoped and almost expected her to be thinking about their relationship. They hadn't really had any time to discuss anything and he wanted things to get off on the right foot with her. He knew what could happen if one party to a couple came into the relationship with fanciful expectations and when things were different than what they had wrongly surmised, it all but doomed the pairing.

David thought it best to interrupt the thought process before it got off to a bad start. "Alice, tell me what you are thinking."

She turned toward him, "I was just thinking about this last week, but mostly about us. I don't know what 'us' is or what you want it to become. We will be in different homes, not like being in the suite next to each other and I just was trying to process what your ideas might be."

David took her hand and looked into her eyes, "Alice, all of those things, questions, and anything else you want to know will be discussed and answered, but not here or now. Just think of this as a lovely few days and the beginning of us getting to know each other." He was being as honest as he could be with her right now, but he knew she would still want to pursue the subject. "Once we are home we can take as long as you want to get to know each other and by the end, I think you will find you will like the journey as well as the destination."

Alice knew it was no use to speculate and decided to wait for more information from David. She had enough to keep her busy for the next couple of months anyway. She had her aunt's cottage to sell, she had to find a place to live, and there was the estate which she wanted to do more work on while she still had everything fresh in her mind.

She smiled at David and agreed to not rush. "I have the cottage to sell and I need to find a home for me. I've lots to keep me busy."

David was glad to see her focus had moved from him and the 'us' question but he worried about the fact she might choose the wrong place to live. He would have to talk to her about that, but not right now. No, now he just wanted to finish his breakfast and maybe take a nap while he was still several thousand miles from his responsibilities at the hospital, his parents, and could have Alice within his reach.

They went through the customs at the local airport and David got a taxi to take first Alice to the cottage and then himself to his condo. He helped Alice take her bags into the cottage and kissed her long and deep. He tweaked nipples and whispered in her ear, "I'll be back shortly to welcome you home properly." She sighed and he knew when he checked her that she was very wet.

Alone at last she shed her dress and put a robe on while she unpacked, sorted the laundry, and checked the messages on her answering machine. When everything was back where it should be she showered and dried her hair before braiding it to sleep. By the time the phone woke her it was almost six in the evening.

David was calling and he greeted her with an invitation to dinner. He would be there at seven to get her and hoped she would be ready. She assured him she would be.

Dinner wasn't fancy but it was something other than French or Italian. They did see Paul Rossi out with a young woman but after he smiled at her and scowled at David, he led his date from the restaurant when they finished their dinner. The steaks David ordered were good and when they left, he took her back to the cottage.

They were barely through the door of the cottage before he had her dress off and had put her on the bed. His clothes landed on a heap in the middle of the floor and his hands were caressing her body. She ran her hands through his hair as he began the magic with his tongue. She was close to climax quickly and he pushed her over into a toe-curling orgasm which vibrated through her body for several seconds.

She knelt on the floor beside the bed and took his fully erect cock into her mouth. Between using her two hands to stroke his shaft and massage his balls, she pulled him as far as she could into her mouth and released her hand to try to take him deep down her throat. He had his hands in her hair and face-fucked her until he came and deposited his cum in her mouth.

He laid back on the bed and she rested her head on his groin. Both were sated and David shortly pulled Alice onto the bed so they could lay down together. He held her in his arms and gently caressed her breasts and sucked first one nipple and then the other. He had plans for those breasts of hers but many things would come before any of that could happen.

It was well past midnight when David woke up and realized he was still holding Alice in his arms. He never intended to spend the night with her, in fact that was one thing he didn't want to have happen. Things could get out of hand rather quickly if he were to do that and the one thing he didn't what to happen was to spoil Alice before she willingly gave herself to him. No, it was time for him to leave.

The next morning Alice was still naked with only her bottom half covered. On the kitchen table was a note from David that he would be busy for most of the day at the hospital but he wanted to have dinner with her that evening at six. "I'll bring the food and wine."

Alice got a lot accomplished. The laundry was done, several bags of her late aunt's clothes were taken to the Goodwill store, and some of the things she was putting in the estate sale was set on the side to be priced by the ladies who were to conduct the sale. The only disappointment was the call to her real estate agent.

Julie Burrows had been in her undergraduate class. They had known each other from high school, but she ran in a large group of popular girls who seemed to have the dating of the football team as their main goal. Alice and Evie had never considered guys, especially jocks, as being anything more than a distraction from where they wanted to be scholastically and professionally. True, neither of them had gone to the prom, homecoming, or any of the other events besides debate or advanced language and math classes.

"Alice you really need to look a bit further out or raise the amount you want to spend," Julie counseled. "The available properties are not that plentiful and those that are on the market have prices out of your range. If you could just bump it up another twenty or twenty-five thousand it would open several more opportunities for you."

"Look Julie," Alice said, "I understand what you are saying, but I don't want some huge place that I can't take care of myself. Three bedrooms and two baths is my limit and if I have to go a bit further out, well, then let me know what you have, but I'm not going any higher."

"Okay, I'll send the listings over to you and look through them. Let me know if you see something you like. You know we can still go condo. I happen to know of one that will be on the market soon and it might be great for you. It has private parking and a couple of other perks." Julie wrapped up the call with a promise to get more info on the condo and the new listings out to her.

Alice looked over the listing as she prepared to have dinner with David. She knew he liked her in dresses or at least a skirt and button up top. She wondered about the no panties or bra thing when they went out, but at home it didn't bother her as much. If he would just say what was going through his mind about them it would help her feel more comfortable about everything.

Promptly at six David parked in front of the cottage. He came to the door but his hands were empty. What about the food? There wasn't anything in the house to cook but if she had known he would forget his promise to bring dinner she would have had something made.

"The food is in the car and we don't want it getting cold so hurry! We're going to my house to eat. I have something to show you." David hurried her out the door and once in his car, drove to a quiet residential area and parked before a large older home.

DAVID'S HOUSE

Alice looked at him questionably, "I thought you lived in a condo near the hospital? This place is huge for just one person or is this your parent's house."

David laughed, "no, this used to be my Uncle Maurice's place until he died and then his widow lived here for a couple of years until she went to stay with her sister. He left it to me and I use it sometimes. I just thought it would help me explain a few things to you. I know you have questions and after we eat, we can talk as long as you want."

He took the bags of food through to the kitchen. There was a lit fire in the kitchen fireplace which made the room warm and cozy. The bags of food were opened and David sat the meal on the big kitchen table while he told Alice where to find the dishes and utensils. He brought out the wine goblets so Alice knew he must not have a surgery in the morning.

Everything looked so good and there was a lot of it. Both of them ate sparingly and when they finished David told Alice where to find the things to make coffee for them. He sat before the fire and watched her as she worked. The light from the fire caught the highlights in her hair and her eyes sparkled in the glow. David liked what he saw and knew he wanted that more than ever, she was the one he wanted to grow old with, to take as his sub or slave and live in peace with for the rest of his life. But first, she had to want the same things.

It would not be about a vanilla relationship. He didn't do the boyfriend thing or settling for part of his vision but not all of it just to have her. No, this was an all-in kind of life. If she couldn't accept what and who he was, he would most regrettably have to let her go.

After she served the coffee, he sat her down beside him and began to tell her who he was and how he lived. He knew she would have a lot of questions, but asked her to let him finish before she asked them. "I am hoping some of them will be answered as I tell you about myself."

He told her about Uncle Maurice and what he had taught him as well as what he learned from Auntie Lala. At one point he told her there was a dungeon in the house and he would take her there to show her what it was. He began to tell her how he lived and what he wanted in the person he knew she could be. "I don't do boyfriend, dates, or many of the things you might get with someone else, but I can promise you that you will be loved and cherished, you will grow in the relationship. When the time is right and we have advanced to a permanent relationship, I would want you to live with me full time. I can also see the possibility of marriage in the future, but that is quite a way down the road."

David went on, "now, ask me some of your questions."

Alice was deep in thought. It was almost more than she wanted to take in. The first thing, though, to come to mind was Dr. Salek's daughter. "Is this," she used her hands in a sweeping gesture that encompassed the room, "what happened with Salek's daughter?"

David looked in her eyes, "No Alice, she was the single time I tried to live a vanilla life. I never told her about this and don't know what her reaction would have been if I had. Besides, I've already explained her to you."

For the next hour David continued to answer her questions. Finally, she asked to see the dungeon. David took her to the locked door and pulling the key from his pocket, he opened it and turned on the lights.

The dark green walls, heavy dark dungeon furniture, and the racks of whips, floggers, canes, and various other paraphernalia hanging from hooks on the walls could be daunting at first sight. Chains hung down from the ceiling, a four-poster bondage bed sat at one end of the room and two St. Andrew's Crosses were also in the room. A large cabinet held nipple, labia, and clitoris clamps as well as cuffs for ankles, wrists, and waists. A spanking horse, bondage table, stocks, and cage rounded out the room.

David took Alice by the hand and led her to each piece of furniture or examined the various items hanging on the walls so he could explain to her what they were used for. "Do you mean you want to do this stuff to me?" The fear in her voice made her speech quiver. "I don't think you have the right girl, I'm, uh, oh jeez, this is just not what I thought you uh, um, no, just no." Alice left the room before he could stop her.

"Alice, please, let's talk," David said as he locked the door and followed her. He found her sitting in front of the fire in the kitchen, staring at the flames, and holding her purse in a firm hug. David sat beside her, "Alice, look, I didn't mean to scare you away, but I wanted you to see the dungeon so maybe you would understand something of what my life is. We all have our secret lives, some live them as daydreams or fantasy and others, like myself and the other Masters/ Dominants who I am friends with, know who and what we are and live accordingly. This is not a full-time part of this lifestyle, its but a small part of it, but it is a part that is me."

"You have to understand, I have spent years discovering who and what I am, how I want to live, and the kind of person I want to share that life with. You are the one I want, you are the one I believe has the capacity to live as my sub and one day, you may even consent to giving yourself to me as my consensual slave." Had he told her too much or is it just that she needs time to process what he is telling her? Has he been so wrong and she is not the one for him? With every fiber of his being, he believes she is the one, but how to let her see this?

"Alice, I will not beg you. I don't think that is what you would want me to do or something you would respect me for in the long run. No, what I do want to do is continue to talk to you, communication and honesty are cornerstones of this kind of relationship. I want to know what you are thinking, I want you to talk to me and I would also like you to listen to what I have to say. This is not something I have come to lightly; I truly think you would be happy with me in this lifestyle." Was she hearing him, really hearing him or was it only something she was suffering through until he could take her home? "Please, talk to me Alice."

She shifted in her seat, looking him in the eyes Alice said in a whisper, "why do you want to hurt me? What have I done to you that I'm to be punished?"

David let his breath out, he moved to her and took her in his arms, "oh my little Alice, I don't want to hurt you and you have done noting that I could punish you for, that is not what this is all about." He held her and could feel her softly sobbing. He took her purse from her and set in on the chair. Raising her face to his he kissed her eyes and tasted the saltiness of her tears. "My sweet, sweet girl, don't cry, please. Talk to me and tell me what your fears are so I can alleviate them."

Haltingly at first she began to spill out a jumble of fears, some triggered by seeing the dungeon and other by the recent losses of first her aunt and then the fact her closest friend was still in Italy. He sat her down on his lap and she continued to talk, the fear of being alone, having to move and not knowing where she should go, even the decompression of having finished her degree and not knowing where to go from that achievement. David let her talk and learned a lot about her as she did.

When she had finally seemed to unload all of her concerns, David suggested she tell him what one thing upset her the most in the dungeon. He wanted to see if he could ally her fears for just one thing and hopefully show her it all wasn't so scary. He had been stroking her hair and holding her in his arms. He whispered in her ear, "tell me sweet Alice, let me show you there is nothing in that room you need to fear." Alice had the same reaction to him she always did when he whispered in her ear. Hm, her body was still responsive, this may turn out okay, he thought to himself.

"The bed," she whispered back.

David picked her up and put her on her feet. Without a word he took her by the wrist and led her to the door of the dungeon. Unlocking the door he said, "if, at any time you want to stop or feel uncomfortable just say red. We use a color system, green for go, yellow for this is getting too intense, and red for stop. Remember that, I am not a mind reader and if you don't tell me, I can't guess at what you want."

Alice nodded. David stopped her, "Alice, that was a yes or no question, not a nod, 'yea', or 'uh'. Can you please give me an answer?"

"Yes, yes I understand on both instances." He led her into the room to the big four-poster bed that had eye-bolts strategically located for bondage purposes. He had her take off her dress and put it on the sofa nearby.

"Please sit on the bed while I get some things from this chest." David returned with a blindfold, ankle and wrist cuffs, and some ropes with quick connectors woven into the ends. The cuffs were padded and would not hurt her skin and the blindfold was the same as those used in the finest spas. He put the cuffs on her and had her lay down on the bed. He used the ropes to open her legs and bind her arms. She lay spread-eagle on the bed and he put the blindfold on her. He put a sultry song to play on the sound system and adjusted the volume.

Immediately he felt her body begin to tense. He leaned over and whispered in her ear, "do not be afraid little Alice, I want you to open your mind and feel what I'm about to do to you." He knew it was the anticipation which would play in her mind and he knew if he checked her now, she would be wet for him. David removed his shirt and slipped into a comfortable old tee-shirt and a pair of work-out pants that tied at the waist. He also laid out the toys he would use on her.

When he was ready, he straddled her chest and gathered up her mass of beautiful hair. He did a lose braid that he secured with a zip-tie. He got off of her and picked up the velvet glove he had taken from the chest. He leaned over and softly growled in her ear. Immediately she tensed but then he took the glove and caressed her body from feet to neck. He loved looking at her and this was a wonderful opportunity to see all of her laid out for his pleasure.

Her nipples hardened under his attention and when he took his mouth and sucked each in turn, felt shivers go through her. He caressed her pubic area and inner thighs then leaned in and licked at her labia with his tongue. He exchanged the glove for a long peacock feather. He tickled her nipples with it and ever so lightly stroked her lips and pubic area. The last thing he wanted to try on her was the horse-tail flogger he had. He didn't strike her with it but simply caressed her skin from her feet to her hair. Lastly, he used his mouth to bring her to orgasm while he kneaded her breasts. The results were more explosive than any she had reached with him before.

He released the cuffs and put a blanket over her as he held her on his lap. He removed the zip-tie from her hair and it spilled over them like a screen. David knew he needed to give her time to recover from the intensity of the experience. It could take anywhere from a few minutes or much longer. He should be able to sense by the way she rested in his arms when she was ready to talk to him again.

After holding her for more than twenty minutes he felt her breathing change. She was coming out of it. He lifted her face to his and he kissed her deeply. "So, sweet Alice, how was your first experience in the dungeon?"

Alice looked him in the eye and whispered, "very intense but very enjoyable. I could learn to love that."

He stroked her hair, "my sweet pet, this lifestyle is not all floggings and spankings, we have rules, protocols, and rituals. But that is for another day, right now I think I should get you home."

Alice began to protest, "but what about you? You gave me pleasure can't I do the same for you?" She slid to her knees in front of him and reached up to pull his cock out of his pants. He used his hands to stop her.

"Alice, I will tell you when I want you to do that. Right now, it is time I take you home." He stood up. "I'll lock up here and you put your dress on. I still have to put the fire out in the kitchen. Meet me there."

She wasn't quite sure if he was angry with her or what was wrong. He saw her hurt look but decided the sooner she began to understand that it was up to him and not her, the sooner she could begin to know how he wanted her to behave. Tonight, was simply the beginning of a long journey for both of them.

House Rules

More and more Alice and David would meet at Maurice's old house. David gave Alice a key and she became familiar with the kitchen and the old master bedroom. It was on her second visit to the house that David took her to the room where his uncle had died and where he and his slave had lived for so many years.

The restraint ropes were still at the foot of the bed. In the big walk-in closet, he showed her the cushion Lala had used to 'recenter' herself from the world outside the house to her place as Maurice's slave-girl inside the house. David patiently explained it to Alice.

"When my uncle first met Lala, she was a nurse. She continued to work outside of the home until he was diagnosed with cancer and then she stayed at his side full-time. It was devastating to her when he died. She had not just lost a husband, which is bad enough, but she had lost her Master. The bond between any successful Master and his slave-girl goes much deeper than most marriages ever reach."

"She would leave the house and go to her work as a nurse supervisor in a local nursing facility. Many times, she worked twelve on, twelve off for four days and then had three days off. Every time she would come home from work or even just out shopping, she would greet her Master in a formal way and then ask his permission to go to her special place in this room to change from outside to inside.

She told me she would change not just her clothes, but while she was doing that, she was remembering who she was to her Master and why she had chosen to give herself to him."

"If there was someone else in the house, like if I was visiting between terms, she would put on a housedress that buttoned up the front. If, however, she was alone in the house or my uncle was here, she would put on the leather cuffs and heavy collar of a slave and not wear any clothes."

Alice looked at him, "why was she naked? Didn't she get cold?"

David laughed, "this house has fireplaces in almost every room and Uncle Maurice had no problem paying a heating bill to keep his slave warm. No, she wore no clothes because that is how her Master wanted her. He wanted to have full access to all of her anytime he wanted. The buttons on the house dress were so he could get to her without having to rip her clothes off."

Alice stared wide-eyed, "you mean so he could have sex with her anytime he wanted?"

David pulled her to him, "Alice, I have told you about communication and honesty as being part of the bedrock of a successful D/s or M/s relationship, but the other three pieces to this are affection, intimacy, and yes, sex." He kissed her and then whispered in her ear, "we have been working on the communication/honesty, I think we have the affection, and we are working on the intimacy. I've told you before that it is up to you to tell me when you are ready for the last part, the sex." He felt her squirm as he kissed her again.

He rested her head against his chest and stroked her hair. "I will wait for you, but I want to have all of you to enjoy. By now I think you know how much you mean to me and how much I want you with me forever." He kissed her again before he led her to the bed. He helped her out of her dress and this time had her kneel before him. He took his fully erect cock from his pants and she opened her mouth to receive it. He told her to put her hands behind her and to let him guide her though to his orgasm. He took her hair in both hands and began fucking her mouth. He deposited his cum in her throat and was still amazed she enjoyed swallowing it so much.

He pulled her up to kiss her and could taste some of the saltiness of his cum in her mouth. "I think this is a perfect time to show you the ritual for going to bed." He instructed her to stand at the end of the bed and open her legs to the widest they would go. Next, she was to bend at the waist and putting her arms out in front of her, lean on the bed with her ass and pussy both fully visible. "Every night before bed, you ask permission to go to bed. You come to the room, do what you need to in the bathroom, then you get into this position so that I can inspect you." He walked around her at the bottom of the bed while she was bent over. "This way, you show you are totally open to me, that there is nothing you are hiding from me, and I can decide what I want to do to you before we sleep."

David caressed her bare ass cheeks. "I may decide you need a spanking, or once we are sexually active, a good fucking in the pussy or maybe even the ass." He laughed, "don't be so shocked, when I said I wanted to use all of you, that includes your ass, but don't worry, it won't be before I have trained you in how to prepare your ass to be fucked. For now, I want you on the bed, lay down face up, spread your legs for me."

Alice quickly complied with his instructions. David put the cuffs on her wrists and ankles then fastened one of the ropes at the end of the bed to an ankle cuff. He also put a blindfold on her. "I want you to open your mind and feel what I am about to do to you." He took nipple clamps and put one on each erect nipple. She had very sensitive breasts and he wanted to heighten the sensations. They were adjustable and he put just enough tension to keep them on but not enough to cause pain, that would come later. Thus prepared, he began.

He used the sound system in the room to play a piece of music that featured African drums. Softly and slowly the drums began a hypnotic beat but as the sound-track played the drums got louder and faster. He took a soft crop from the chest in the closet and began lightly tapping Alice's inner thighs to the beat of the drums.

He never stayed in one place on her body moving the crop from her inner thighs up to her breasts, stomach, and pubic area. He was careful not to strike her exposed pussy or labia. He didn't want a mistake with a toy to damage her virginity. As the music built in sound and intensity his strokes also increased. He began to concentrate on the outside of her closed pussy lips. When the drums were beginning their final crescendo, he replaced the crop with his mouth Opening her so he could use his tongue to bring her to climax, she exploded in orgasms almost as soon as his mouth made contact with her clit.

He held her as the intense waves roiled through her whole body. He popped the nipple clips off her nipples which only added to the intensity of the orgasms. He removed the blindfold and could see she had her eyes closed while she savored the powerful feelings.

For a young woman to have this strong a reaction to what had just happened to her was unusual. David was looking forward to the day when she would give him her womanly prize and he could teach her body to respond on a sensual level that he thought would be epic. Just the anticipation of her responses to him made his cock throb and his balls hard. Only with great self-control was he able to resist the urge to have her completely right on this bed, immediately.

He rolled her on her side and covered her. David undressed and held her naked body against his until the urges he was feeling got too intense. He kissed her and re-dressed. He lay next to her but did not put her against his body. One hand rested on her hip. It was just enough contact for her to feel he was near but not enough for him to lose his self-control. When she finally roused later in the night, they both dressed and he took her back to her cottage before he went to his condo near the hospital.

As things progressed with David, she also had the cottage to sell and another place to live had to be found. She and David talked about many things, but her sale of the cottage and subsequent move to another place was not one of the topics. This is why his bringing up the subject seemed strange to Alice.

Alice had seen several properties with the real estate agent she had searching for a place to live and that same agent was also in charge of selling the cottage. None of the things she had seen interested her or they were too far out or didn't have parking for her Dad's Shelby. Alice spent a considerable time on the phone with Julie, her agent, but came away very frustrated with the call. The cottage was as ready to be sold as she could make it and she needed to move but she needed a place to go.

Alice was going to be cooking for David at the old house and after getting the groceries she would need she let herself in and began preparing the meal. David arrived before it was finished and he surprised her with some flowers and another lesson in her training to be his sub. He felt there was some tension in Alice and he told her to sit and tell him what was on her mind.

"Alice, we have to have open and free communication and I feel there is something that is weighing on your mind. Tell me what it is and maybe I can help ease your thoughts." He sat next to her on the couch where he could hold her hand while she talked to him.

She sighed, "I'm having trouble finding another place to live. My agent, Julie, has shown me several places, but there hasn't been any of them I want to put my money into. They are either too expensive, too far out, or don't have parking for the Shelby. I can't really sell the cottage until I have a place to go."

David squeezed her hand ever-so lightly. "My dear Alice, come live here. There is plenty of room, a garage for the Shelby, and I won't have to worry that you're not in a safe place when I'm not here." He had thought about having her live in the big house before but this might just be the perfect way to accomplish his goals. "I know we have not decided positively on making this relationship permanent, but if we were ready to do it in the next year or two, it would just mean another move for you and having to put your next house up for sale."

"This would be perfect. With you here, I could come whenever I can to see you and we can continue your training. We still have much to cover and even tonight, I intend to teach you some formal protocols and rituals about how you are to greet me when I arrive. But we will get to that after we talk about your housing dilemma." He noticed her look away, hm, something he was saying was bothering her. Best to cover that before they continue.

"Alice," David said, "what are your thoughts on what I've just said?"

She looked down, thinking, finally she made eye contact. "You have never stayed the night with me, never shown me where you live, and I feel like I'm a part of your life you want to keep on the side and secret. It's hard to buy your professions of affection that I am so important to you when I feel like you only want me to be a part-time part of your life." A single tear ran down her cheek as she again bowed her head.

David tried not to sound angry or emotional when he spoke to Alice. "Look at me." Slowly she raised her head and looked into his eyes. "That's better, I don't like talking to the top of someone's head. Now, let's get something straight." Although he was trying not to be as gruff, it wasn't working and he could see tears glistening in Alice's eyes. He reached out and stroked her hair. "I don't spend the night with you because I want to fuck you so bad it is all I can do to muster up enough self-control to stop myself from ravishing you. I haven't shown you my condo because I do nothing there but sleep, shower, and change clothes. It's more camping than real living."

He continued, "as for this feeling you have of me hiding you away like some secret, you have been seen with me more in public since we met than I've been with my own mother. I'm not really a going out kind of guy. I like the peace and quiet of an evening at home with you by my side or playing with you in the dungeon. There are also our talks and your training."

He kissed her, "I am so looking forward to the day when I can take you out and show you off to my D/s and M/s friends as my girl. Eventually, we will invite them here and you will get to meet other girls who are subs and slaves. I am and always have been so proud of you and who you are. I would never hide you away or try to keep you as a secret."

"Oh, and another reason I haven't taken you to the condo is I am in the process of having a house built. It's pretty far out, but when it's finished, I will want you to see it. Someday, if our relationship progresses, I will want you to live there with me full-time." Alice was surprised, this was the first she was hearing that he was building a house or planed on living someplace other than near the hospital where he worked.

"How can you be so far out and not near the hospital?" If open communication was going to work, it had to flow both ways. "Is it close enough to get to the hospital in an emergency?"

David laughed, "I see this has opened a whole new line of discussion. Suffice it to say I don't always plan on being tied to this same hospital. I've been toying with opening my own practice and treating people from both Green Valley and Oakland. It's still just a thought, but the house is something that means a great deal to me so it's not really about the hospital or work."

He saw her questioning look. "Years ago, my Uncle Maurice found a wonderful place to picnic. It looked abandoned, overgrown, and was just land and a lake, but Lala would pack a picnic lunch and uncle would drive us there for a picnic near the lake. After lunch, he would play with Auntie Lala. He would have her take off her dress and tie her to one particular tree. He would flog her, whip her, and spank her until she dropped into subspace. After, Maurice would take her down, wrap her in a blanket and very lovingly hold her and care for her until she came out of it."

It was David's turn to be emotional. "On his death-bed Uncle Maurice told me to find out who owned the property and buy it. He also asked me not to cut down Lala's favorite tree." David's eyes glistened too, "It wasn't until recently that I was able to find it and buy it. Seems it was held in an old estate and was finally revealed during the probate process. I had them start building before I met you and Evie in Paris."

David cleared his throat, "now, check the dinner and if there is time, I want to teach you the protocol and ritual for how I want you to greet me when I come in."

With a place to live, as least temporarily, the move out of the cottage into the big house was done in just a week. The following week a couple from Ohio bought the cottage as a retirement home. Before the month was out the closing documents were signed and the money for the sale were added to the monies from Aunt Dorie's estate.

Living in the big house was convenient, however one thing bothered Alice. She was not allowed to move into the master bedroom but another one down the hall from it. While it had a nice bathroom attached, it still made Alice feel as if she was being relegated to a minor role in the house.

She finally decided she would ask David about the unsettling state of her residency in the house. Alice had worked for a couple of hours making a lovely dinner for when David came home. Part of the protocol he had taught her was the ritual of how to greet him when he arrived from outside the house. He said he would always call her when he was about to arrive so she could be prepared.

Alice's cell phone received a text message from David that he would be at the big house in about ten minutes. She turned off the burners on the stove, checked the roast in the oven, and went to the closet in her room to take off her dress. Naked except for some soft house shoes, she went to the front door to wait for David to arrive.

David parked his car in front of the house and she knelt in front of the door but back far enough so it would not hit her when he opened it. She then stretched out her arms as far as they would go in front of her with her forehead on the ground, much like a kowtow position. She waited for David to unlock the door, come in, and then acknowledge her. She then assumed a formal kneeling position where she would stay until he decided what he wanted to do with her.

"Beautifully done" he said as he patted her on the head. He put his bag and keys on the hall table and stood in front of her. He unzipped his pants and withdrew his erect cock. "Suck it princess," was all he said. Alice had been instructed by David when he taught the protocol that he would decide if and how he would use her when he came home and as a good sub she would comply without hesitation.

So far it was all good. However, he told her during the instruction that much like going to bed, he might tell her any number of things and she needed to do them promptly and happily. "This is all part of how I live."

During one of their long talks, he had told her that she was not the first girl he had considered as a sub. "The ones I had before had all had some training when I met them. They were people I'd met at local BDSM clubs or through lifestyle friends. For one reason or another none of the three had worked out. Once they would ask to be released, as one girl did, I would let them go, but that was the end of the relationship, there was no me chasing after them or them changing their minds and wanting to comeback. This is a one-shot deal. The other two just didn't seem to be in a position to go the distance of a long-term relationship and I let them go."

Alice swallowed his cum and he put his cock back into his pants and zipped his fly. "Come girl, dinner."

She rose and went to the kitchen. It took only minutes to put the food on the table and then she waited for David to give her a nod that meant she could sit down. "Tonight, I have a surprise for you. I've written to Auntie Lala and she is going to come stay here next weekend. I want you to have the guidance of a woman who was a superb sub and then slave-girl to my Uncle Maurice. I think she can give you a lot of information that might help you in your growth and decision to become my sub."

"Thank you, I look forward to her counsel. There is also another matter I would like to discuss." David nodded toward Alice to continue. "It's about the bedroom where you want me to sleep. Why can't I sleep in the master bedroom?"

David put down his fork. "Alice my pet, there may be some nights when I am too tired to go to my condo to sleep and I will sleep in the master bedroom. You can't sleep there unless it would be on blankets on the floor. I just can't take the chance that I would fuck you before we were ready." He hoped this would be the last of it but it didn't look like it was satisfying her.

"Alice, when Lala was my uncle's sub then slave, she didn't sleep on the bed with him all of the time. She had her bed at the foot of his bed and slept on the floor like a good girl. He would sometimes ask her to come lay beside him, but not all of the time." David continued, "I have not decided about your sleeping with me, and before you ask, yes, they were married but that was secondary to their D/s and M/s relationship. At the very end, actually just a short time before he died, he allowed her to lay beside him and she was holding him when he passed."

Now it was David's turn to bow his head so Alice didn't see his eyes glisten with emotion. He didn't want anyone to see his soft side, but she knew it was there. Anyone else would have taken her virginity long before now. She might be an ingénue when it came to sex and the actual sex act, but she also was learning when David was using his iron will-power to avoid deflowering her. This endeared him to her.

She often wanted him to go further, but hesitated to say so for fear of the unknown. She also noticed the slight change in the decision being only 'hers' to a 'we' deciding when she would be fully sexually active with him. Alice knew he wanted to fuck her and now she wanted it too.

David regained his composure and the conversation turned to preparations for the visit of Lala. "I want you to prepare the room next to yours. The one you are in was hers but since you are there, we will put her nearby. Also, I will get some fresh flowers for her." He told Alice to give him a reminder about the flowers the day before Lala would arrive.

Dinner finished, she took a few minutes to clean up the kitchen, put the dishes in the dishwasher, and put the leftovers in the fridge. She then made them both a coffee. Sitting before the fire in the kitchen was the place David seemed to like the most outside of the master bedroom and dungeon.

David took her hand and led her to the dungeon. "Tonight, I want to spank you. I've held off on this kind of impact play before, but I think you're ready." He unlocked the door and put cuffs on her and turned the sound system on to the same African drums he'd used before. Next, he sat on the sofa and had her kneel before him. After placing the blindfold on her he whispered in her ear, "remember your safe words. I have been looking forward to using you all day today." He felt her squirming and pulled her across his knee.

He began by rubbing her beautiful ass cheeks. As the music began to build, he started to lightly spank first one side and then the other, caressing her as he went. The faster and harder the drums beat his hand kept time with the music and the spanking became more intense. He still caressed her but not as often. He also growled in

134

her ear a couple of times which seemed to make her wetter. As the music was about to reach a crescendo, he lifted her onto the couch and buried his face in her pubic area so he could use his tongue to make her cum. Again, it was an all-body shaking orgasm. If she was available to him fully, he would have put her on the bed and fucked her or restrained her on the spanking bench where he also would have fucked her.

David wrapped her in a blanket and held her in his lap. When he removed the blindfold, he could tell she was in subspace and he would hold onto her until she came out of it. Shortly after she revived, he gave her some water to drink and carried her to the bedroom. "I think you can do the inspection in your room tonight because you should go to bed. I will stay with you for a while, but will sleep in the master bedroom."

The inspection routine showed her ass was still red from the spanking. "Do you want to see? Go look in the bathroom mirror." Alice went into the bathroom and looked at the red marks on her ass. She was happy to see them and now knew about the pain/pleasure such an exercise could provide.

"Oh, I like the look!" she said. She came back into the room and again assumed the inspection position at the end of the bed. Tonight, David simply placed a kiss on her ass and told her to get into bed. She still had the cuffs on and he took off all but one on her right ankle.

"From now on, I want you to become accustomed to wearing cuffs in the house and the one ankle cuff to bed." He took the connector at the end of the rope tied to the foot of the bed and attached it to the cuff. "I also want you to become used to being restrained when you sleep. Now, if you need to go to the toilet or you need to get out of bed for an emergency, you can take it off, but put it back on when you return to sleep." He smoothed her hair back. "I want you to do this even when I am not in the house. I also think you should be naked in the house full-time except when we have visitors."

Alice looked into his eyes, she was beginning to realize that she was in love with this man, but although he had spoken of 'affection' and 'intimacy' he'd never said anything about love. Was that not allowed in a D/s relationship? She wanted to ask him but wasn't sure of how to start that particular kind of conversation. What if he said he didn't see her as a love interest but only as a service person? No, she didn't want to risk finding out she was little more than a servant who did the work and sucked his dick.

Alice finished the last of the cleaning and straightening of the house, put the flowers in a vase on the dressing table in the guest room for Lala, and checked the casserole in the oven. David had gone to the airport to pick up his Auntie Lala and should be arriving any moment. Dressed in a simple shift dress with buttons down the front, Alice was nervous that she would remember all of the protocols and rituals she had been taught.

She heard the car door close and voices on the front walk. Alice opened the front door and bowed low to David and curtsied to their guest. Lala's smile was warm and any trepidation Alice had felt about the visit melted immediately.

Turning to David Lala said, "She is as beautiful as you told me and I see you have been working with her on various greetings but," turning to Alice, "I would simply ask David permission to hug you as a greeting!"

Alice blushed and hoped she hadn't done the wrong thing by curtsying to Lala. David however, smiled down on her and tweaked her nose, "she's coming along but we still have a way to go and is still not quite sure about all of this," he made a sweeping motion with his hand to indicate everything around him, "and I don't think it's fair to her to ask for any until she knows exactly what "all of this means."

Lala hugged Alice and David instructed her to show Lala to her room before returning to finish the dinner. Although his auntie was older than the last occasion he had seen her, she was still the slender woman who had been his uncle's slave. Her hair was greyer, she wore her sixty odd years well. Her demeanor and gracefulness were still very much apparent.

They had talked on the ride from the airport, mostly about Alice and what David's hopes were for the relationship. Never before had he seemed so taken with a girl and he'd never asked or wanted anyone's opinion of his choice. She had asked him some very pointed questions, a habit she had gotten from his late Uncle Maurice. The most direct was his intentions towards her.

Lala had reminded him that "your uncle, my dear Master, was adamant that you not take on the ownership of either a subordinate or a consensual slave until you had first mastered yourself and knew how and what you wanted in your life. I know at the end he told you that you were ready, but I know you were aware of the fact he never stopped working on his mastery of me or our relationship even to the moment he was about to die and he allowed me to lie beside him and hold him as he left me."

"Being a good Master is not for the weak, inattentive, or lazy. You should know this, but please be very careful with your girl. If you are truly committed to having this girl, make sure to not cut corners with her training or you could damage the relationship in the long term." She continued, "my Master was able to see something in me I didn't realize was there but with patience, training, and perseverance he led me to a wonderful life. It was not always easy or smooth. If I can help your girl I will, but she has to want to accept you, your vision, and your way of living, I can't force her into it no more than you can." She dropped her gaze and blushed slightly at a long-ago memory.

David sighed, "it doesn't get any easier, does it, having him gone?"

Lala's eyes glistened, "not even a little. I've been approached by other masters who are either slave-less or were wanting to add another to a poly household, but what Master and I had was only for us, I could never call another man Master."

"Do you miss the play in the dungeon though," David asked. "I know uncle could often get you into subspace, do you miss that?"

Lala shook her head, "Master could do things to me I would never have believed possible and it was for him, what he wanted, and he took me along with his desires. Most of the time it was followed by sex. There hasn't been a man for me since he died and I don't want one."

Lala helped Alice in the kitchen and dinner was soon served. Alice had tried to do it all herself, after all, Lala was a guest, but she would hear none of that. "If you will let me, I want to help," Lala said.

Dinner was lively. David and Lala talked about old times and people they both knew, many who were in the lifestyle. Alice mostly listened unless a question was asked of her directly. She like Lala and was looking forward to being able to talk to her about the kind of life David was telling her he wanted. She had also been given a list of books, by David, on the subject of the D/s and M/s lifestyle and had many questions to ask her about what she had read.

David had an early surgery so after enjoying coffee with Lala and Alice he asked Alice to join him in the master bedroom so he could do an inspection before he left her to visit with Lala. Alice took off her dress and took the formal inspection position at the end of the bed, after which he ordered her to her knees to suck his cock. Once finished he told her to dress and reminded her of how she was to sleep. "Don't forget you will wear the right ankle cuff and restraint." David caressed her cheek and kissed her, "good night my pet. I'll call tomorrow when I can come back."

David left and Alice put her shift back on. She was in time to tell Lala good night and then went to the kitchen to clean up the coffee. Looking around the kitchen she saw that Lala had already done the work. It was time for her to go to bed.

Alice had the coffee and an omelet ready to slide onto Lala's plate when she came down to breakfast. They chatted about nothing in particular until they both got to their second cup of coffee. "Tell me Alice," Lala began, "what are your thoughts about what David and you are doing? I'm here to answer any questions you might have about it from the perspective of a sub/slave. You must have questions."

Alice thought for a few seconds, "I have days' worth of questions. I didn't even know this was something, this lifestyle, until a few months ago. He has explained it, how his Uncle Maurice introduced it to him, his study and work to define who and what he was and wanted, but it's all so new and strange. He gave me books to study and while he told me that each of the author's was telling what their vision and interpretation of the D/s, M/s lifestyle was, it did give me something to try to learn from."

Lala reached out and patted her hand. "I was the same when my Master found me. I was a floor-nurse at the local hospital and he would come to visit a friend of his who was a patient. He was always watching me and told me later he could tell right away that I was the one for him. I wasn't so sure though; we must have talked for over eight months before I agreed to even let him try any of his things on me."

"Uh, I know you were married, but what about love? I don't think I could ever be just a housekeeper who kept food made, the house clean, let him spank me, and suck his dick forever. I don't think the life of a servant is what I want but he keeps telling me this is so much more. He's told me a lot of things about affection, communication, honesty, and intimacy, but never anything about what they would mean to us."

Lala studied Alice's face. "There was something you left out, sex, what about sex?"

Alice blushed, "I, uh, um, well, I'm a virgin. In the beginning he said he wouldn't take that unless I asked him to but recently, he has changed that to when 'we' want it."

Lala thought about what Alice had just told her. "How do you feel about David? Take the D/s out of it, just how do you feel about him?"

Alice didn't have to think on that one, "I believe I love him. I know I do but it was not a 'love at first sight' kind of thing. At first, he was simply an annoyance, someone who just wouldn't go away no matter how much I asked him to. Then I realized I would look for him and was a little sad when he wasn't there. I guess the turning point for me was when my aunt had a stroke and he was going to do a surgery on her heart to try and save her life. As it happened, she died before he could do it. I guess it was the way he was with me then that made me see him in a different light."

"After Aunt Dorie passed," Alice paused to control her emotions, "he would come and check on me. At the time there was another man who I would have dinner with off and on but he didn't affect me, physically, like David does. He just needs to whisper in my ear or even growl and pull my hair and I have to change panties." Alice looked over at Lala, "oh, my, I hope I haven't shocked you. I'm sorry for being so, uh, well, so graphic about this."

Lala laughed, "don't worry about it! I want you to let me know everything, if I know what is and in fact, isn't going on with you and him, I don't know how I can help. The more open, the better. Besides, I'm sure he told you about the dinners and dungeon play-parties we used to have here with other Master/slave or Dom/sub couples in the group." Alice nodded, "well what do you think the slaves and subs would talk about when we were preparing dinner or clearing up after?"

Alice shrugged her shoulders, "I don't know, what?"

"We never talked about our Master or Dom in any way that would bring embarrassment or ridicule upon them, but we did talk about some of the feelings we had and every once in a while, a sister sub or slave would just need a friendly ear or knowing shoulder to lean on. Being in the lifestyle, we understood a lot of what the others were going through, having done it ourselves." Lala did want to impress one very important point upon Alice, "but the person to whom you need to talk to and be open with above all is David. You will get your greatest strength and support from him."

Lala stood, "what do you say we get that roast in the oven and we can talk while we work? I know you have many questions and I will try my best to deal with each one."

Alice got out the meat and vegetables so they could get to work on David's dinner.

Alice had pulled one of the books David had asked her to read out of the library/office and showed Lala something she didn't understand. "You see, this man talks about Emotional Monogamy but Physical Sharing. Now as he describes it, he only loves his slave/wife, but he will participate in other Doms/Masters wanting to share their slaves or subs with him sexually and in addition there would be a time that he would share his slave/wife with another Dom or Master, sexually. All the while they were both in love with each other.

Sex without affection/love." She slid the book over to Lala so she could see the passage to which she was referring. "I don't think I could do that; I mean even the idea that he might pass me around to his other lifestyle friends is the stuff of nightmares."

Lala shook her head, "you know, that was one of the same things that bothered me when I read it. When I asked my Master, well he was then my potential Dominant about that he told me there would be no sharing, either way. He also reminded me that this was one man's view of M/s, but he didn't ascribe to it. He did say the author was one of the best on the overall subject and that is why he had me read his books."

Alice was relieved, but then remembered Lala was talking about her Master, would David look at 'sharing' the same as his uncle? She was going to have to find out. "Another thing is the discussion of the contract. David has told me that his lifestyle, vision, and the way he lives is not up for debate. He would not modify these aspects of his life for anyone and if, when the time comes for me to make the ulti-mate decision to ask him to accept me as his, I should not agree to all of what he wanted, he would deny me and send me on my way."

Alice looked down and when she again looked up at Lala her eyes glistened with tears. "I don't want to lose him, but if he is unbending on everything, what is left to negotiate in a contract? I'm afraid that I might ask for something he wouldn't want and he would turn me away." Alice shook her head, "I don't think I can live without him."

Lala got out of her chair and sat next to Alice on the sofa. She hugged her and stroked her hair while Alice cried. "There, there sweetie, don't be afraid of that. What it means is there are some things that you can change. For example, in my contract there was a clause about no urine, blood, or scat would be used in play. I had a bad experience when I was in nursing school with another girl who was a lesbian and I didn't want to be forced into sex with another woman. Also, knives, needles, and any kind of medical play was off the table. My Master agreed to these things so readily that I think he would never have done them either."

Now it was Lala's turn to tear up. "He did have one clause that I wished I had never signed on for; he had a sentence about me never getting pregnant or having a baby. At the time I signed the first contract I didn't think I would ever want children; later however, I brought up the subject and he would always point to the contract. When we renewed it after five years and I asked to become his slave, I thought we would be renegotiating the first contract for Dom/sub, but that wasn't the case. When I again asked him, he punished me for nagging him about it."

Alice shivered, "punished you, how? Did he do that often?"

Lala smiled at her. "If there are no consequences for bad behavior, not following the rules, rituals, or protocols he wants you to live under, or just some bratty tantrum, why would we live as we do? My Master would punish me in various ways, sometimes from restricting my orgasms, or even just letting me know just how much I had displeased him, but in severe cases, like my nagging him about having a baby, he would whip and cane me. Whips are alright, but canes, no thank you." She remembered the pain when it hurt to sit down for a week. "I don't know how David would punish you for something, but if you can help it, best not to test him."

Alice grimaced. "He hasn't disciplined me as yet. He said if he hasn't taught me something he can't expect me to know it or do it. If, however, he has taught something then it is best I do it right and remember it. I think part of what he is doing is giving me a chance to see if this is even something I want to do and a way to live with him."

Lala smiled. "Tell me something, do you have a job outside of the house or is this old thing," she gestured at the room, "the extent of your world except for grocery shopping and an occasional dinner out with David?"

"Hm, first off, since I came to live in this house, David and I have not been out to dinner or really anywhere else together." Lala looked surprised at that, but Alice continued. "I don't know what he has told you about me, but I graduated several months ago, with honors, with a Master's in Middle Ages History. I moved in here after selling my aunt's cottage which I inherited. I've also inherited a rather large estate from my parents which I actively manage. I use the office space and WIFI in the library to do the work."

Lala smiled, "He hasn't told me but I think that is wonderful. The best slaves/subs are women who are accomplished, well educated, and have interests outside of the home. Contrary to what many people may think, we are not doormats who just lay down and get walked all over." She laughed, "one of my best slave-sister friends was a lawyer and senior partner at a big legal firm in a town near here. She had been with her master for over thirty years and they had three children, all well-adjusted and probably never knew the M/s relationship of their parents."

She held Alice's hand, "tell me, why do you manage this estate on your own? Doesn't it take experts to take care of such an enterprise?"

Alice laughed, "not at all. Mostly it is in the form of stocks, bonds, and some precious metals. There is the cash that my aunt left me and from the sale of her house. I was going to use that to buy myself a place to live but David talked me into coming to live here. Now it just sits there and earns a little interest. I guess I could use some help, but I'm not too sure where I would go or who I would talk to about it."

Lala thought about what she had said. "Have you considered having your own office outside of the house? I know there are a couple of companies that rent out office space with the use of a secretary, conference rooms, and some other amenities also available." She saw the questioning look on Alice's face. "For your own emotional health and wellbeing, you need something outside of this house and this lifestyle where you can be 'vanilla' and part of the larger community. For some women it's hobbies or charity causes that gives them time away from their life with their Dom/Master. It is good on two levels; it gives you some outside interests and when you come back home it makes the life you have chosen all the more real."

Lala continued, "I worked at the hospital, first as a floor nurse and then as a supervisor, for most of my time with my Master. It wasn't until he was diagnosed with cancer that I left work and gave him my full-time attention. Master was spiritually with me every day from the beginning, even at work, but at last I could devote all of my waking hours to him. I wouldn't have had it any other way."

Again, Lala's eyes started to tear when she remembered her life with her beloved Master.

Now it was Alice's turn to comfort Lala, "I only wish I can find this kind of life and peace with David."

Alice and Lala talked for most of the time Lala was visiting in the big, old house. David had work that kept him away but he always came for dinner and to inspect Alice for the night before he had to leave. The time away from Alice and their life, however brief together, helped solidify for David just how much he wanted Alice in his life full-time and forever. He was anxious to have Lala tell him what she thought of Alice when he would take her to the airport.

The day Lala was to leave, Alice made a lite lunch for them. The plane wasn't until the late afternoon and David came to eat with them. The two women cleaned up the kitchen and sat with David for a cup of coffee before he would be taking Lala to the airport.

When Alice said goodbye to Lala there were hugs and tears from both. "You have my address and email so don't hesitate to contact me anytime. My phone is still an old landline so if you call and I'm not there, just leave a message and I'll get right back to you." Lala told Alice, "I think you'll do just fine but anything I can do to help, just let me know." Alice closed the front door and Lala was gone.

A few hours later a call came from David that he would be home in about ten minutes and expected to be greeted properly. "I want you naked and ready to be used when I get home."

Alice hurried what she was doing, went to her bathroom to check that her hair was combed out like David liked it, and took her formal position near the door to greet David. She heard his footfalls on the front stairs and slightly shifted her butt so it was high enough in the air and her pubic area fully exposed, just like he had taught her.

He opened and closed the door, looked at his girl on the floor in the position he wanted, and ordered her to his knees. "Kneel" was all he said. Eyes downcast, Alice waited for him to speak to her or give her another command. She heard him drop his keys on the front hall table, he put his case beside them, and came to stand in front of her.

"Look at me." Alice raised her head and looked into his eyes. "Finish dinner while I shower," and David turned and went to the master bedroom to change and shower before supper. Alice went to the kitchen and tried to think about what his behavior was telling her. He didn't ask her to suck his cock, he didn't kiss her, things he might have done at other times, but she wondered if something she had said to Lala had caused him to be angry with her.

Alice spent the time in the kitchen finishing up the dinner and going over what she and Lala had talked about that might cause angst. David spent his time in the shower replaying the conversation he had with Lala on the way to the airport. David had a lot to think about.

From the time the car rolled down the driveway until he took her bags out of the trunk at the airport, Lala and David talked about Alice and what his intentions were toward her. Lala did most of the talking with only an occasional question from David. Lala didn't hold back, nor did he expect her to.

"David, what are your intentions? Have you told Alice or are you expecting her to guess at what you want from her and how you look at your relationship? This girl loves you; I mean really loves you but is afraid to say so because she doesn't know if all you want from her is someone to do the work in the house and suck your dick!" Lala wasn't letting up. "She said she gets affection from you, but wanted to know if being a servant who fulfills your needs in the dungeon while sucking your cock is what she wants for the long term."

"She's a virgin, Auntie, and I am trying my best to not take that from her until she asks me to take it. As for the intentions, I do love her and have since I first met her. I want to marry her and make her my sub, but before I can talk marriage, she needs to ask to be my sub." David continued, "I want to know she is ready to make that commitment before we would be married. I don't want her to agree to something knowing marriage would be part of it until she knows for sure." David had known a couple in which the man had told the wife, while he was training her, that they would be married if she became his sub and she agreed to be a sub only to ask to be released from that part of the relationship after he had married her. Her ultimate goal was marriage and pretending to accept being a sub was what she thought she had to do to get what she wanted. The marriage ended badly. David did not want that.

"David, you are going to have to talk to this girl about your feelings. My Master was very good at letting me know what his feelings were towards me or on any other subject. It didn't diminish his mastery of me nor make him vulnerable in my eyes." She chuckled, "if anything, it made him all the more my Master. I knew exactly where I was with him and never doubted his love and affection for me, even unto the last."

"Now, as for the virgin issue. I think if you asked her, told her how you feel, she would give it to you more than willingly." Lala looked over at David's profile, "I know you and my Master were not blood relatives, but you remind me so much of him. Of course, he was over fifty when he first began talking to me and I was just turned thirty. I would have loved to know him when he was younger, but I cherish every day we had together." Lala brushed away a tear, "don't lose precious time. If you love her, tell her, if you think she is ready, let her know what you intend your life together to be, and if you ask her, I think you are both ready to add 'sex' to the other parts of the basis for a solid relationship."

David concentrated on his driving and what his auntie was saying. "The thing about the, uh, virginity. I've been able to control my urge to be fully sexually active with her for this long, well, I was thinking I might like to keep that for our wedding night or even when I collared her."

Lala looked over at him, "David, we do not live in the Dark Ages! You will be the one to open her, whether it is tonight or on your wedding or collaring night, there will be no one else that she is sexually active with so why not let her decide when it will be. If you ask me, she would give herself to you tonight if you asked her."

David toweled off and put on a pair of casual pants and tee-shirt. He looked at himself in the mirror and secretly smiled. Hm, if Lala was right, he would take Alice to the dungeon after dinner and see where the night led. He didn't have any surgeries or appointments until tomorrow afternoon so he would have a glass of wine with dinner or maybe, after they played in the dungeon, a coffee and brandy by the fire in the kitchen. Yes, the coffee and brandy afterwards but no wine for dinner. He wanted to be completely clear-headed when he played with Alice on this night.

Dinner was on the table and after he sat down, he nodded to Alice for her to take her seat. She was doing everything he was asking of her, but tonight he wanted to see if this was going to be for the long-term or only a short, kind of play-acting thing that would not serve for his wants into the future. He had to know before he let her know the depth of his feelings for her. The trepidation over making a serious mistake had to be conquered but he had to know.

Dinner finished he stood and told her, "Clean up the dinner things and meet me in the dungeon. It has been sometime since we played together and I feel a need to try something new with you. I will use you tonight."

Alice smiled. Just the words, "I will use you tonight" made her so wet. Being naked she was afraid the moisture from her pussy would run down her leg, but she didn't dare bother with it, he liked her this way. She flew through the dishes and when she got to the door of the dungeon, he told her to come in and close the door. He stood by the St. Andrew's cross that was on one of the short walls. Next to it hung a selection of floggers, whips, crops, canes, and paddles. He motioned for her to put a blindfold on when she was at the cross.

David attached her to the cross with her back facing outward. He put the same type of drum music on but it was different enough that Alice would not be able to anticipate where he would be taking her in their play. He leaned in close and whispered in her ear, "I love you my pet and want you to do this for me. I need to know if you can do for me what I need. Do you understand?" With no hesitation Alice said yes.

He started out by giving her a few hand spanks on each butt cheek followed by caresses. He switched to a soft flogger that he played up and down her back and buttocks then switched to a crop that he used to concentrate on her butt, the sides of her breasts, and her pussy. All the while, the music was building and the pace became harder and faster. Each of these he had used on her before but now he took a harder flogger and began using on her and except from some moans and an occasional 'ouch', she was doing okay. The last thing he wanted to try was the whip.

David took the braided leather whip off the wall, extended it and popped a loud 'crack' near her ear. He saw her tense and knew he needed to sooth her before he began. He caressed her and whispered in her ear how much he loved her and how well she was doing. She started to relax. He took the whip and laid a strip across her butt. A sharp 'ow' escaped from her lips but David caressed her and stepped back to take a second stripe which he laid just above the last. The third and last one caught Alice in the upper back and the end of the whip hit the side of her breast but Alice didn't move or make a sound.

David put the whip away and wrapped a blanket around Alice before releasing her from the cross. He removed the blindfold and could see she had slipped into her happy place in subspace. His heart burst for this girl. She had endured everything he had wanted from her and did it in a way that few that he knew could have done this early in their training.

His Auntie Lala was right, he needed to have a serious discussion with his girl, but not tonight. Tonight, he would hold her until she dropped out of subspace and then he would put her to bed where she could sleep as long as she wanted. He would stay the night in the master bedroom and tomorrow morning when Alice was rested and refreshed, he would talk to her about the future.

Alice stretched and released her right ankle from the rope that bound her to the bed. She smiled at the cuff on her ankle and put the other cuffs that were on the bedside table on her wrists and other ankle. Looking at the time, she hurried through her morning bathroom routine when the door to the bedroom opened and David came in carrying a tray with coffee and croissants.

"Good morning little Alice. Are you still checking my handiwork from last night? Come here and greet me properly." He smiled at her and had her turn around so he could see the faint marks and a few welts he had put on her the night before in the dungeon.

Alice dropped to her knees and David took his fully erect cock out of his pajama pants so she could suck it. She loved this and he was still amazed at how expert she was at taking all of his cock into her mouth and the seeming joy she showed as she sucked and swallowed every last drop of his cum. She smiled up at him while licking him clean.

He pulled her up to him and kissed her long and hard. He could taste his saltiness in her mouth and on her tongue. David wanted all of her but that would have to wait on the outcome of their talk.

David handed Alice a cup of coffee and the two sat on the bed with the tray between them. "I think it is time we had a serious talk about our future, don't you," he began. "Last night you made me very happy and I think we answered the question of if you can take what I want to do to you, but how do you feel about what I did? I need your honest and open answer, don't give the answer you think I want to hear but your true thought and feeling on this." God his naked girl was beautiful he thought.

Alice set her cup and partially eaten roll on the tray. "I know what you did last night was for you. Before, I was scared that what you wanted to do was something I would not be able to endure, but I opened my mind and leaned into the pain because I knew you wanted it and my only wish was to make you happy. I don't even remember all of it, but my butt sure does!"

"You don't know how scared I was that I was going to safe-word you. That is something I never want to do because I know you will always keep me safe and never do anything that will hurt or damage me." Her eyes started to tear. He took the tray and put it on the table.

David came back to the bed and took her in his arms. "Alice, Alice, we need to talk about our future. Are you ready for that?"

Alice whispered a yes in his ear. If she ever thought the effect he had on her only went one way, she hadn't learned to read his body. He felt the first stirrings of his cock at her touch, the scent of her hair, and the whispered answer in his ear began to affect him. If he wanted to keep her a virgin, at least for the next hour or so, he needed to move this conversation off the bed and into another room.

David picked up the tray, "come girl, let's finish this in the kitchen."

Alice went to the bathroom to rinse out her mouth before she left the room. David was already in the kitchen with the coffee and rolls sitting between them. While he talked, he held her hands in his. "From the first time I met you I felt something for you. Acting so quickly and saving my mother the way you did impressed me greatly but the more I saw of you I began to realize that I had an affection for you. Granted, when I saw Paul Rossi hanging around you it was difficult, he was competition and I had to ask myself, competition for what and the answer I got back was for you."

David took a sip of coffee before he continued. "I didn't want him around you because I wanted you. I was in love with you and the idea of another guy was more than I could take. The more I thought about it, well let's just say I probably fell in love with you the moment we met." He gave her hands a little squeeze before he continued. "The present arrangement we have is that you would live here until we decided if you would be my sub. Everything, I have taught you you've learned well. Your potential as my permanent, life-long sub is not in doubt, but you must agree that it is the position you want."

"Alice, I would like you to think about this very carefully. I'm not going to put a timeline on how long you have to give me an answer because this is probably one of the most important decisions you will ever make. I think you know what is at stake here and it must be your decision." David leaned back in his chair and Alice put her hands in her lap. He could tell by the way she was fidgeting she had something she wanted to say. He gave her a slight nod and a wink.

Alice smiled. "David, you know me, I've kept nothing from you. Last night's play was something I had feared but you showed me there was nothing of which to be afraid. You have shown me a life I never knew existed. While I do remember my parent's marriage, those memories are marred by the fighting and disagreements they would often have over the silliest of things. That is something I don't see happening to us. I want to give you the power to make the decisions in my life and our relationship." She paused to try to read his face but got nothing.

"David, I still need to have some interests outside of the house and after my talk with your Auntie Lala, she has given me some wonderful ideas on how I can do that." She looked around the kitchen, "while this is a large and nice house, this can't be the extent of my world. I want you to be my world, but I also need to feed my intellect with something more than cooking, cleaning, and sucking your cock."

David chuckled, "I want you to have something outside of the house, as long as you know who you are inside the house and who you belong to wherever you are, I think we are on the same page." He leaned forward and took her hands again. "Alice, I know I've always told you that the matter of your virginity was up to you, but another part of this, well, If you agree to be my sub, that would mean you are giving me control over your body. What if I would then decide I would want you to stay a virgin until we would be married? Would that be a problem for you?"

Alice blushed. "It depends on how long I would have to wait for the wedding night!"

David got out of his chair and pulled her up to him. He kissed her deeply and when he let her come up for air he whispered in her ear, "I don't think it would be a long wait at all, but you're saying you want me to fuck you? I need to hear you say it so there is no question but that it is your desire."

She whispered in his ear, "David, I want you to fuck me!"

He scooped her up in his arms and took her to the master bedroom. He put her down in the middle of his unmade bed and stripped off his pajama pants. His cock was hard and fully erect. "Fuck the wedding night, I want you now!" he saw the look on her face. "I will be as gentle with you as possible." He hesitated only long enough to put on a condom.

He settled himself between her open legs and using his mouth, moistened her clit and the opening to her passage. She was very wet and he put a little of his spittle on his cock before he began. Slowly he rubbed her clit with the end of his cock and then parted her pussy-lips with it. Next, he slowly began to push into her then withdraw.

All the time he was looking at her face for any signs of pain. "Open your eyes my sweet. I want you to see the ecstasy you bring to me when I cum inside of you."

When he finally entered her all the way he felt the resistance of the hymen as it gave way to him. Alice grimaced slightly as he went past it, but he could see and hoped it hadn't hurt her too much. When he looked down at his cock going in and out of her pussy, he could see faint traces of blood on the condom. She had given him something she could never take back.

He shifted their position until she was on top of him and he was pushing up into her from below. David finally climaxed and she lay beside him for several minutes. "You are amazing. I will always remember this day. Did I hurt you? Tell me what you feel?" David pulled the condom off and put it in the trash beside the bed.

"It didn't really hurt and I could tell you were hitting some spots that were very pleasurable, but nothing like when you use your tongue on me." She blushed from the memory of the last orgasm he had given her.

David rolled off the bed and went into his bathroom to get a warm cloth to clean the blood from Alice. "Here, "he said as he handed it to her. "She took the rag and cleaned herself. There were traces of blood, a testament to her virginity on the washcloth.

He took it from her hand and used his hand to bring her to orgasm. Both were spent and he held her in his arms while they recovered. Finally, with a resounding slap on her ass he told her it was time for him to get ready for work and for her to do her work. Sex had been the missing part of the foundation of their relationship and now it had been added.

Alice looked forward with excitement for David to return from the hospital. The dinner was ready to be served when he called to tell her he was on the way. She was in the kowtow position waiting for him to unlock the door.

David came in and told her to kneel. He smiled down at her and put his case and keys on the hall table. Reaching down he told her to stand and come with him. In the kitchen the table had been set and a fire warmed the room.

One end of the table was empty and he told her to lay across the table with her ass in the air and her legs open as wide as possible. He sheathed his erect cock and spit on his hand so he could lube his maleness and checked Alice if she was wet enough so he didn't hurt her. Finding her very wet, he entered her and braced himself with a hand full of hair and one of her hands pulled back to him. He fucked her until he came and then, pulling out turned her around and put her on the sofa in front of the fire. David used his mouth to bring her to orgasm while his hands pulled her nipples and rolled them between his fingers.

"We are going to have to talk about your breasts. I want them so badly. If we ever have a baby, I want to share your milk with him. Until that time, we may have to work on making some of our own." Alice loved what he was telling her. She would be happy to have milky breasts from which to feed her man. First though, she had to decide if this was the life she wanted. She wasn't quite there yet, but it was still something she was thinking she wanted.

A slap on her ass brought her back to the present. "You can tell me what you are thinking over dinner. Hop to it," he laughed.

While they ate, she told him what her thoughts were and how she was feeling. One of the issues had to do with sex. "I have seen the porn videos you recommended and it seems like the woman always has an orgasm when the man is in her. So far, I have had some sensations, but nothing close to an orgasm. Is there something wrong with me? Do I satisfy you?"

David took her hand, "first off, porn movies are mostly make-believe. As for you satisfying me, you are more than enough for me and satisfy me completely. Will it get better, absolutely! As we learn each other's bodies we will learn what will make things even more satisfying." He pulled her into his lap. "There are things I can do that will make your ears ring, but you have just been opened, give it time."

She rested her head on his shoulder. In his ear she whispered, "will you use me again tonight?"

He pulled her around so he could look in her eyes. "Have I created a sex-crazed girl here?" She blushed, "I understand, but you must remember," he continued, "I'm the one that determines when and where. Right now, you need to finish the kitchen dishes and then I want you in the dungeon, I'll see you there."

David had Alice bound to the spanking/fucking bench in the dungeon. The red leather upholstered and padded piece of furniture had adjustable kneeling pads and the height of the main bench piece could also be raised or lowered to put Alice at just the right place to either suck David's cock or for David to fuck her pussy or ass. After making the proper adjustments, he had her lay on the bench and attached her cuffs to the O rings located in the various binding points. This time he put a heavy leather collar on her neck and attached it at the front of the bench.

All the time he was doing this he was talking to her. "I usually don't use impact play on successive nights, but in this case, I want to use you on the spanking bench. I've not used it before because I didn't want to take the chance I would accidently interfere with your virginity but now that is no longer an issue. Tonight, is the night when you will get to use this bench for me."

As he worked, he also caressed her and kept telling her what a good-girl she was. Finally finished, he put the blindfold on her and took time to change into his dungeon play clothes and put the music on. He wanted to start opening her ass so he could use it when he wanted but tonight was not the time to begin something new. No, tonight would be all about doing something he had been wanting to do since he first met Alice and she kept defying him.

For David, she needed and deserved a good spanking followed by an equally deserved fucking. He's wanted to from the start and tonight she would get and he would give it. The music he chose was not African drums but classical guitar music which also had a growing urgency and increase in volume but also exuded passion like the passion he felt for Alice.

Before he began, he whispered in her ear and saw her squirm as his words made her pussy wet. He stroked and rubbed her ass cheeks before he began spanking her with his hand and he continued to caress her as he continued. His handprint shown red against her white skin and he stepped back to look at his handiwork. Next, he took one of the 'slapper' paddles off the wall and continued his work on her ass.

The music continued to build and the strokes of the paddle were replaced by one of David's old belts, a toy he was particularly fond of for spankings. However, as the last frantic cords of the music began to thunder through the room, he had put a condom on his erect cock and prepared to enter his girl's wet pussy.

Slamming into her he could feel the walls of her passage constrict around his fully engorged cock. He hadn't felt that from her before but it made his enjoyment that much more and before he was really ready to end this, he shot his cum load into the condom. Pulling out of her he stripped off the condom and went to her head and put his cock into her mouth. She sucked the last of the cum from him, licked and swirled her tongue around the head, and sucked his balls.

David went to the wall and removed a vibrator from the charger. He hadn't used one on her but tonight would be a great time and she was in such a great position. Carefully he lubed the top of the vibrator head and found her clit. He took his other hand and with two fingers, proceeded to finger-fuck her while the vibrator brought her to orgasm. Her reaction was to buck and pull against the restraints, proving the reason for her being be restrained was to keep her from harming herself.

He quickly removed the restraints and the blindfold. David wrapped her in a blanket and held he on the bed in the dungeon for over an hour while they kissed and whispered to each other. Finally, David sent her to the master bedroom so he could do an inspection of her. Tonight, he would do nothing more than look at his most recent handiwork and remind her to cuff herself to the bed before she slept. He would sit with her until she slept but he couldn't spend the night.

Alice looked at the marks David had left on her the night before. Aside from the bed in the dungeon, she now had a new favorite piece of furniture. She blushed as she remembered the spanking followed by the fucking, but she also enjoyed David's use of the vibrator on her. When David had left the night before, he told her he would be busy most of the day and wanted her to do whatever she needed to do but he would call her about five to tell her when he would get home.

She dressed in a very smart suit. One of the things David had told her almost from the start was how he wanted her to dress. In the house, by themselves, it was easy, she was to be naked except for the cuffs. He didn't like her to wear pants unless it was something that couldn't be done in a skirt or dress. If she was going outside, he wanted her to be without panties or bra, to sit with her bare ass on whatever seat she was on, and when she was with him, she had to keep her thighs open so he could feel her sex whenever he wanted. This suit, however, had a pencil thin skirt which was not conducive to baring her ass on the seat. In place of that, she would have to use a half-slip to keep from getting pussy-juices on the skirt and also remember to buy suits with fuller skirts.

The white silk blouse she wore with the navy-blue suit was perfect for where she was going. Lala had mentioned she should have something outside of the house and today she was going to look at temporary office space. She wouldn't make a decision on leasing it until she had discussed it with David, but it was time she made managing her finances on the estate a more professional endeavor.

The modern eight-story building where the offices were was impressive. The company that leased the spaces occupied the second and third floors while a couple investment and venture capital firms had the rest of the building. Alice's appointment was at eleven and by three minutes till she was at the receptionist's desk. She didn't like to be late.

Before the appointment, while she was parking the car, she received a text from David telling her he had made her an appointment with a woman gynecologist at the hospital to discuss birth control. He told her he had wanted to talk to her about it last night, but was so swept-up in the play he didn't get the chance. That appointment was for one in the afternoon. She texted back that she would be able to make the appointment.

The young man who showed her the offices available for lease was very nice and a good salesman. She took the information and left. There was a café in the lobby of the building and she decided to get some lunch before going to the afternoon commitment.

Alice sat at one of the small tables near the back of the café and ordered a salad and unsweet tea. She was about half way through her lunch when a familiar voice called her name. Looking up she saw Paul Rossi with a group of men about his age enter the restaurant. Paul waved and she smiled back.

Paul broke away from the group and came to Alice's table. "Alice how are you; it's been ages since I've seen you. What are you doing here?"

Alice didn't ask him to sit down but looked up at him and smiled. "I'm doing wonderful. Today I was looking at some temporary office space in the building but I'm not sure it's right for my purposes. How are you?"

Paul noticed she didn't invite him to sit and it must mean she was still with David Khoury. "I'm doing good. How's David?" That was one way to find out if he might have a chance with her.

"David and I are doing just fine. Evie is in Florence studying and will be there for several more months." Alice was sure now this was not the building for her. "Do you work around here?"

"Sure, just upstairs. I work in a venture capital firm. Exciting work." He turned to leave, "you know, we can still be friends."

Alice looked at him, "no Paul, I don't think we can, I'm with David and I don't think that will ever change."

Paul rejoined his work-mates and Alice left for her appointment at the hospital. She would not take an office in this building but there were other places where she could get temporary office space.

The visit with Dr. Riley was interesting. She had Alice undergo a complete exam, she took blood and urine samples, and then they sat down to discuss contraception. "Well, you're not pregnant right now so we can begin to use the contraceptive you might feel most comfortable with or that fits your lifestyle the best." Dr. Riley had a chart on the desk and they discussed each one.

Alice knew this was something she needed to decide upon during that visit. "Tell me more about the injections."

Dr. Riley smiled at her. "That might be your best choice. For the first six months I want to give you twice-monthly injections here in my office. If I'm out then my P.A. can give the shot. After the that time, we can go to every six months. If you were to decide you wanted to get pregnant, we would stop the shots and start you taking your temperature each morning to determine when you ovulate. Usually that happens after being off the medication for a few months." She tried to read what Alice was thinking but her face was a blank.

Finally, Alice replied. "And how long after the first shot can I have unprotected sex?"

Dr. Riley smiled to herself. Another of David Khoury's girls. She had been the doctor for his other live-ins but it had been over two years since the last one was in her office. She hadn't really thought about him until he called her office for her in the morning. So, he's got another one, hmm, she didn't look like the others, maybe this one was different. "I would like your partner to still use a condom for the first week, but after that it should be okay. If, for some reason, you have intercourse before that without a condom, take the 'plan B' pills right away. Some people call them the morning after pills, but don't wait until the morning if you can help it."

Alice nodded. "Okay, can you do the shot now?"

Dr. Riley smiled and left to get the injection tray. When the medication had been administered the office clerk brought her an appointment card for the next dose and Alice left to try to see the other office building, she thought might have offices available for short-term use.

Naked except for the cuffs on her wrists and ankles, Alice waited for David in the kowtow position by the front door. She heard him walk across the porch that led to the front door and by the time he had opened it she was wet in anticipation of his arrival. "Rise pet."

David put his keys and bag on the front table and came and tweaked her nipples. "Did you see Dr. Riley like I asked you?"

"Yes, I did." Alice replied, eyes still facing David and unmoving from the formal stand he had ordered her to take when he told her to rise.

"And what did you do? Did she start you on something?"

"Yes, she started me on a shot." Alice replied.

"How long must I use a condom when I fuck you? You know I don't like condoms so I hope it is not long." He smiled.

"One week. Then you will not need a condom to keep me from being pregnant." Alice said in an even voice.

"Excellent, then come with me." David could smell the wonderful aromas coming from the kitchen but he wanted to use his girl first and then again, it there was time, after they ate.

David unlocked the dungeon door and bid Alice to enter. "On the bed," he ordered. He stripped off his outside clothes and put on a pair of comfortable dungeon clothes. From one of the hooks, he took down some leather restraints. He put them on her thighs and secured them to her calves. Next, he opened her thighs to the maximum and pulled her to the end of the bed.

He spoke to her in a low voice and finished the restraints. He put a blindfold on her and put on a low, sultry instrumental as background music. He took his hand and caressed her breasts, played with her nipples, and he continued to tell her that he wanted to use her and what he wanted to do. He could tell she was getting more and more aroused as he began to play with her clit and tested the wetness of her pussy. He brought her almost to orgasm but pulled away just before tipping her over the edge.

Finally, when he felt she was ready, he put a condom on his erect cock and entered her. As he slid into her, he used his one hand to pull her nipples and the other to circle her clit with his thumb. Almost immediately an orgasm began to roll through her body. He continued to fuck her while she was orgasming. He kept the stimulation on the clit going until she had experienced at least three strong orgasms. Then he pulled out, shed the condom, and put his cock in her mouth where she sucked him and he fucked her mouth until he came down her throat.

David undid her thighs, removed the blindfold, and released her ankles. He hugged her close to him and smoothed her hair. She rested her head on him and he waited until she could speak. Finally, he kissed her and looked in her eyes. "Tell me what you are thinking my love."

He gave her a sip of water and she began to tell him about her day, the encounter with Paul Rossi, and the doctor's appointment. She ended by telling him about the office space she had seen at the second place she visited. All the time she was speaking he continued to hold her and rock her in his arms. Finally, he told her to go freshen up and prepare for dinner. He would be along once he had straightened up the dungeon.

During dinner he asked her about the office space. "Now you are sure you can get out of it after six months, right?" David knew the new house would be finished and it would be much farther than this old house was to the temporary offices she was looking at that afternoon. Alice assured him that was the case and when he asked her about the exchange with Paul he watched to see if she was giving off any signals which would indicate there might be some latent desire for him, but he saw none.

Once he finished his questions and allowed her to speak about her thoughts she asked if she could say something. He told her to please go ahead. She shifted in her chair and briefly looked down at the table. David began to get a queasy, foreboding feeling in his core. He dreaded she might have made the decision to reject him, his lifestyle, and becoming his sub.

When Alice finally raised her head, she looked into his eyes. "Uh, before I finalize the decision about becoming your sub, there are a couple of things I need to know. Perhaps you can help me with those."

David reached for her hand, "anything, Alice, what do you need to know from me?"

"Well, what about children? Do you want any? Will you let me have a baby or babies if we get married?" She continued to stare into his eyes.

"Alice, if you become my sub we will be married. As for children, yes, I want them and yes, I would only want you to have them.

I will enjoy putting a baby in your belly and watching you grow a son or daughter for us. I do think we should not rush into children but I would like some. And, remember, I will be the one to make the decision when and how many we will have." He saw her start to relax, but not all the way which told him there was something else bothering her. "What else do you need to know?"

She let a long breath out, "when your Auntie Lala was here, she and I discussed several things. Two things have been bothering me." David motioned for her to go on. "Well, the first is the idea of sharing." She started to tear-up and he understood she had a fear of it.

David squeezed her hand, "if you are mine, you will only be mine. I don't share and if you are worried about me sharing myself with someone else, I don't do that either." He could feel her relaxing but knew there was still another big concern standing between them being together or him having to let her go.

It hit him then, 'let her go', he couldn't do that, he mustn't do that, but if he had to, he would. There were no compromises in this. He didn't live vanilla and as much as he loved and cherished her, he would keep his word. What was the last thing keeping her from being his sub or maybe in the future his consensual slave? "What is the second thing you are worried about?"

Alice gulped, "Lala and several of the books you had me read talked about punishment. She said it might simply be knowing I had displeased you, depending on what I had or hadn't done. But she also told me how your uncle, her master, punished her for nagging. He used a cane on her and, uh, well, uh, she didn't like it at all. I would never want to make you angry or to do something that would make you disappointed in me. Really, I don't think I could ever be a bratty person, but, well, I need to know about the punishment. I know what it is for, I just need to know, uh, how."

"Alice, any of the things I have used on you so far might be used to punish you. It would all depend on the infraction or the intent of your misdeed. The only think I haven't used on you and I usually keep it only for punishment is a particular thin, composite cane." He kept looking in her eyes to gauge her reactions to what he was saying, so far, she was still okay. "If I decide to punish you for something, you will know why. Also, once it is done, it is over with. I won't keep using something against you in the future. Once you have been punished, the slate is wiped clean and we don't talk about it again."

David could tell there was still something, but what it was, well, he would have to ask. "Does this clarify things for you?"

She dropped her gaze, when she looked up again, he could tell there was definitely something else. "I, uh, I need to know how it feels. I need to know if I can take it. Can you show me?"

Punishment was something he didn't like to do but his uncle had stressed that it was necessary to keep bad behavior from creeping into the relationship. If this was something she needed to know then he would show her. He left the table and she heard him unlock the dungeon door. Shortly he closed it behind him and came striding into the kitchen with a slender, long cane in his hand. "This is it. It doesn't look very harmful" he said, "but I assure you it is. There are only certain times when I would use this on you. I might use it for punishment, but like my Uncle Maurice, it is used in the collaring ceremony of a sub, and the acceptance of a slave."

Alice looked at him in wonder, "if you use it for punishment, why when you collar a sub or accept a slave? It that something to be punished for?"

David laid the cane across his lap and took Alice's hands again. "No, my sweet. Those are not times to be punished, but they are the final reminder to the sub or slave about their pledge to be a sub or slave and to impress upon them their commitment to giving up their power to their Sir or Master. For most who enter into this lifestyle the welts this brings up," he nodded toward the cane," are like a badge of honor for knowing they can not only endure but thrive in their new lifestyle." He thought a few moments, "but, if this is the only thing keeping you from a decision," he signed, "then come."

David took her hand and told her to assume the position of bend and brace. She stood with her legs as far apart as possible and bent over from the waist. She braced herself with her hands on her knees. He rubbed her bare ass and saw the fading marks he'd put there over the last few days. He smiled, bruises upon bruises, took a deep breath and then let it out. He whispered in her ear which immediately elicited a response.

The cane made a whooshing sound as he brought it down on her ass. "Count" he said, Alice regained her balance, "One". Another whoosh, "Two". Whoosh, "Three". She didn't cry out but he saw a tear drop onto the floor. He put the cane down on the table and took her in his arms. "I'm sorry, but you wanted to know. It wouldn't be any harder, but it would be more hits, depending on the infraction. For a collaring or acceptance as a slave, eight for the sub and ten for the slave."

He could feel her tears on his tee-shirt. A silent sob shuddered through her body but he was proud of her. She took the use of the cane on her and didn't fall apart, safe word him. or run screaming from the house. He put her on his lap as they sat in front of the fire in the kitchen. It took almost thirty minutes before she could talk.

She wiggled away from him and sank to her knees in a formal kneel. Looking up into his eyes she said, "if you will accept me, I want to be your sub, Sir." She bowed her head and waited for him to give her an answer.